Proust as Musician

Proust
as Musician

BY

JEAN-JACQUES NATTIEZ

TRANSLATED BY

DERRICK PUFFETT

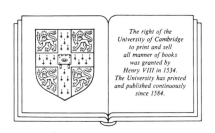

The right of the
University of Cambridge
to print and sell
all manner of books
was granted by
Henry VIII in 1534.
The University has printed
and published continuously
since 1584.

CAMBRIDGE UNIVERSITY PRESS

CAMBRIDGE

NEW YORK NEW ROCHELLE MELBOURNE SYDNEY

Published by the Press Syndicate of the University of Cambridge
The Pitt Building, Trumpington Street, Cambridge CB2 1RP
32 East 57th Street, New York, NY 10022, USA
10 Stamford Road, Oakleigh, Melbourne 3166, Australia

First published 1989

Printed in Great Britain at the University Press, Cambridge

British Library cataloguing in publication data
Nattiez, Jean-Jacques
Proust as musician.
1. Fiction in French. Proust, Marcel,
1871–1922. A la recherche du temps perdu.
Special subjects. Music
I. Title II. Proust musicien. *English*
843'.912

Library of Congress cataloguing in publication data
Nattiez, Jean-Jacques.
[Proust musicien. English]
Proust as musician / by Jean-Jacques Nattiez; translated by
Derrick Puffett.
p. cm.
Translation of: Proust musicien.
Bibliography.
Includes index.
ISBN 0–521–36349–7
1. Proust, Marcel, 1871–1922. A la recherche du temps perdu.
2. Proust, Marcel, 1871–1922 – Knowledge – Music.
3. Music and literature. I. Title.
PQ2631.R63A85213 1989
843'.912–dc 19 88–27535 CIP

ISBN 0 521 36349 7

le parfum persistant des fleurs du passé
And to Christie and David, in friendship

A book could be written on the significance of music in the work of Proust, in particular of the music of Vinteuil: the Sonata and the Septuor. The influence of Schopenhauer on this aspect of the Proustian demonstration is unquestionable . . . Music is the catalytic element in the work of Proust.

Samuel Beckett, Proust (1931)

Contents

Preface to the English edition

The decision to publish an English translation of my book *Proust musicien* (Paris: Christian Bourgois, 1984) was taken at a time when the work of Proust had just fallen into the public domain. In 1987 the famous Pléiade collection began to bring out a new edition of *A la recherche du temps perdu*, a critical edition this time and in four volumes instead of three. With only three exceptions, notably the passage on the Vinteuil Septet, which will appear in the new edition of *La Prisonnière* (*The Captive*) after the present book has been published, all the passages I have analysed are included in the new volume I, which contains *Du côté de chez Swann* (*Swann's Way*) and Part I of *A l'ombre des jeunes filles en fleurs* (*Within a Budding Grove*), along with 900 pages of rough drafts, variants and critical notes. I have taken the opportunity provided by this English edition to update my text, in particular modifying my account of the genesis of *A la recherche* and adding information that has recently become available.

The original book was the result of a seminar on the relationship between the arts held at the University of Quebec at Montreal in 1976–7 and an interdisciplinary seminar presented jointly by the Department of French Studies and the Faculty of Music of the University of Montreal in 1981 and 1983. Warmest thanks are due to the students and to my colleagues Christie McDonald and David Mendelson for their perceptive criticisms at that time.

There are moments in the life of a musicologist or a critic that reward him for having spent long hours on dreary tasks. The moment, for example, when Derrick Puffett, the remarkable translator of this little book, telephoned its author to tell him that, having found in it the answers to certain questions he had asked himself in the past about Proust's relationship to music, he had decided to translate it, without even being assured of a publisher. Derrick will doubtless reproach me for making public what is, after all, the result of private enthusiasm, but it is the only way I know to let my readers understand why I cannot find adequate words to express my gratitude.

Jean-Jacques Nattiez
Montreal, April 1988

Translator's note

The object of this translation is to make the book available to the widest possible readership. All quotations are therefore given in English. The many extracts from *A la recherche du temps perdu* appear in the standard revised translation by C. K. Scott Moncrieff and Terence Kilmartin (*Remembrance of Things Past*, 3 vols., Harmondsworth: Penguin, 1983), based on the Pléiade edition of 1954 (the new edition has not of course been translated); the corresponding passages from the 1954 text are reproduced in an Appendix. For consistency, titles of individual books of *A la recherche* are given in their conventional English form (*Swann's Way*, etc.). However, it seemed better to say *A la recherche du temps perdu* than *Remembrance of Things Past*. The following abbreviations have been used:

C	*The Captive (La Prisonnière)*
CP	*Cities of the Plain (Sodome et Gomorrhe)*
F	*The Fugitive (La Fugitive)*
G	*The Guermantes Way (Le Côté de Guermantes)*
S	*Swann's Way (Du côté de chez Swann)*
TR	*Time Regained (Le Temps retrouvé)*
WBG	*Within a Budding Grove (A l'ombre des jeunes filles en fleurs)*

Four further abbreviations require explanation:

CSB	The Pléiade volume containing *Contre Sainte-Beuve* and *Pastiches et mélanges*, ed. Pierre Clarac (Paris: Gallimard, 1971)
JS	The Pléiade volume containing *Jean Santeuil* and *Les Plaisirs et les jours*, ed. Pierre Clarac in collaboration with Yves Sandré (Paris: Gallimard, 1971)

MPG   *Matinée chez la Princesse de Guermantes* (the rough drafts for *Time Regained*), ed. Henri Bonnet (Paris: Gallimard, 1982)
NE   The new Pléiade edition of *A la recherche du temps perdu*, ed. Jean-Yves Tadié (Paris: Gallimard, 1987–)

In these cases I have made my own translations.

For quotations from other sources, 'received' translations have been used wherever possible and the bibliographical references revised accordingly. All other translations are mine, as is all material in square brackets.

Thanks are due to Esther Cavett-Dunsby, Alfred Clayton and Hugo Tucker for reading and commenting on the translation, and to Monica Buckland and Jackie Scully for typing it.

1

Introduction: Beyond the 'little phrase'

Yet another contribution on the special relationship between Proust and music, one might think. This is, in fact, a topic of research and reflection which returns with pendulum-like regularity in Proust criticism. It is certainly not my ambition to present a synthesis of all that has been written and all that could be written on the subject, but it seemed to me in the light of recent information that a fresh look at the question might be justified. I shall start by surveying the work of my predecessors, in order to define the aims and limits of the present essay.

According to Ingarden, literature constructs a quasi-world. This is particularly true of Proust, whose *A la recherche* reveals a complex, complete and self-contained universe. Like all phenomena of the world, music has its place in it, a special place, as we shall see, alongside society, the emotions, literature and painting. Hence we can study the musical universe of Proust the man (Piroué 1960: Part I, 'La Musique dans la vie de Proust') – drawing on biographies, memoirs, correspondence (Mayer 1978) – and of his work: Georges Matoré and Irène Mecz (1972: 30), using the index in the first Pléiade edition, have identified the names of 170 writers, eighty painters and forty musicians. Wagner comes top of the list with thirty-five mentions, Beethoven second with twenty-five; Debussy appears thirteen times. These figures are probably conservative, for the index does not include adjectives ('Wagnerian'), the titles of works or numbers (*Lohengrin*, the 'Song to the Evening Star') are not listed, and the text contains allusions to specific works or composers[1] that have to be decoded.

It is not surprising, then, that there are so many studies dealing with

Proust's relationship to music: his tastes and aesthetics (Piroué 1960: Part III), music and society in his day (*ibid.*: 45–56),[2] snobbery and the avant-garde, his conception of musical time, etc. Most of these topics have been addressed by Georges Piroué and will not be referred to again.[3]

In Proust, however, music influences the fact of literature itself. In the first book devoted to Proust and music, Benoist-Méchin (1926, repr. 1957) maintains that the majority of Proust's comparisons are of a musical nature (see also Piroué 1960: 169–73). This could only be proved by compiling a complete list, an enormous and patient undertaking: no doubt it would require a team. Milly, in a particularly thorough stylistic study (1975), has tried to show how phrases concerning the composer Vinteuil possess their own unique characteristics. To check this work systematically would be an endless task, for if the Bergotte/Vinteuil comparison were to be convincing one would have to make sure that these stylistic features did not recur elsewhere.[4]

The richness of Proust's vocabulary is well known. The passages in *A la recherche* devoted to music have been the object of lexicographical studies (e.g. Ferguson 1974) and thematic studies (Matoré and Mecz 1972).

In the field of purely literary studies there has also been research, often fascinating, into the genesis of the sections that touch upon the compositions of Vinteuil. The very history of *A la recherche* – to which I shall refer in chapter 2 – is the object of ever more exhaustive investigations, itself a novel upon the novel. Yoshikawa's fine study of the Septet (1979), irrespective of its stated aims, contains a wealth of observations relevant to our subject. Detailed questions of genesis as such concerning the musical episodes in Proust will not, however, detain us here.[5]

All this is just to remind us of the multiplicity of directions and ideas for research on the literary level that have been suggested by the presence of music in the work of Proust. But there is more.

Yielding to a classic temptation in comparative studies of music and literature,[6] critics have sought to trace musical *structures* in *A la recherche*. The title of Part IV of Piroué's book, 'La Structure musicale de "A la recherche du temps perdu" ', is a case in point, even though the author rightly emphasises that he has 'never entertained the idea of demonstrating the correspondence between Proust's novel and music' (1960: 193). Even such a critic as Costil – whose principal article is of unquestionable importance, as will emerge later – does not hesitate to speak of the 'musical construction' of *A la recherche* (1958–9), a phrase which turns out to have a purely metaphorical application: he means construction according to the role played by music in the organisation of the book, something entirely different. Those who have ventured into literal comparison have quickly discovered the pitfalls of metaphor. *A la recherche* has been compared to a symphony (de Lauris 1948: 33), but does the discovery of an ABA structure in passages of the work or in the original plan justify talk of sonata form? The most constant leitmotif in such studies is the Wagnerian leitmotif itself: Matoré and Mecz (1972: 246–54) seem to have listed once and for all everything that distinguishes the specificity of a leitmotif in music from the Proustian system of preparation and anticipation – which is not to deny that Proust is in some respects very close to Wagner, as I shall try to show. Milly, in a more recent book (1975: 72), has postulated an equivalence between the leitmotif and the anagrams that he believes he can discern in Proust's text; but in order to accept the suggestion one would have to be convinced that 'their density shows my regroupings are not arbitrary' (*ibid.*).

However, the favourite theme of studies devoted to the presence of music in Proust, and the one that most fascinates the general public, is the search for sources of 'the little phrase'. Piroué made a reasonably complete assessment of what was known about this at the time when he wrote his book (1960: 173–90). In order to clarify my own position on the matter, it is necessary to supplement his work with some more recent information.

Ever since Painter first published his biography (1966, repr. 1983) it has been known that each of Proust's characters borrows various features from a multitude of real people. And so we can take Proust seriously when he writes, in his famous dedication to Jacques de Lacretelle (in *CSB*:[7] 565): 'Insofar as reality has been of use to me (which is not very much, to be honest), the little phrase of the Sonata – and I have never told this to anyone – is (to begin at the end), at the Saint-Euverte soirée, the charming but ultimately mediocre phrase of a violin sonata by Saint-Saëns, a musician I do not care for.' There is no reason to think that Proust is making fun of his correspondent, since this statement is confirmed by the explicit reference to Saint-Saëns in *Jean Santeuil* (*JS*: 816) and since the Sonata is still attributed to Saint-Saëns in the 1910 drafts of 'Swann in love' (*NE*, I: 909, 911, 913, 918, 935, 941). Proust continues: 'I should not be surprised if, in talking of the phrase a little further on at the same soirée, I had thought of the "Good Friday Spell".' I shall try to demonstrate, later in this essay, the particular role that Proust's interest in *Parsifal* plays in the *meaning* of *A la recherche*. Further: 'Still at that very same soirée, when the violin and piano are moaning like two birds in dialogue with one another, I thought of the Franck Sonata (especially as played by Enesco); Franck's String Quartet appears in one of the later volumes.' Proust thus confirms that he was inspired not only by the inventor of cyclic form – in which the same theme returns from one movement to another of the same work – but also by the connection between two works of the same composer: Painter has shown (1983: 565–6) the thematic connections between the Violin Sonata and the Piano Quintet of Franck, connections analogous to those between the Sonata and the Septet of Vinteuil.[8] Indeed, in 1918 Proust alludes to a quartet, which in the course of the successive transformations of the manuscripts will become a quintet, a sextet and finally a septet. We know from other sources that Proust had noted 'Franck Quintet' (while reminding himself to 'insert another name') in the margin of a description of a concert at Balbec which he did not use (*WBG*, I: 1028). Again: 'The tremolos that obscure the little phrase at the Verdurins',' says Proust, 'were suggested to me by a prelude to *Lohengrin*, but the phrase itself at that point by something of Schubert's. At the same Verdurin soirée it is a ravishing piano piece by Fauré.' J.-M. Nectoux has managed to show, in an exceptionally well-documented article (1971), what the Sonata owed to Fauré's *Ballade for Piano and Orchestra* in its piano solo version. In the pages of *Les Plaisirs et les jours* that are devoted to Mme de Breyves (in *JS*: 74), Proust attributes a function analogous to that of the little phrase to a passage from *Die Meistersinger*: 'She had made it . . . the veritable leitmotif of M. de Laléande.' Finally, according to the direct testimony of Benoist-Méchin (1957: 19), Proust was thinking of the theme of the Andante with Variations which concludes the Piano Sonata No. 32 of Beethoven when he wrote:

[The little phrase] was still there, like an iridescent bubble that floats for a while unbroken. As a rainbow whose brightness is fading seems to subside, then soars again and, before it is extinguished, shines forth with greater splendour than it has ever shown; so to the two colours which the little phrase had hitherto allowed to appear it added others now, chords shot with every hue in the prism, and made them sing.   (*S*, I: 383)

As far as the Septet is concerned, Yoshikawa has catalogued all the composite sources in the rough drafts (1979: 298, 305). If Carnets 3 and 4 are to be believed, Proust was influenced by the 'fixed relation of the elements of the soul in Schumann' and 'the sudden, pathetic grandeur of a phrase by Schubert'. More precisely, the bell-sounds in the Septet (*C*, III: 252) must be attributed to the end of the Franck Symphony (Carnet 3); 'the spirits, the dryads, the familiar deities' (*C*, III: 261) to 'the habitual phrases, the habitual harmonies of Franck' (Carnet 4); the motif of 'the only Unknown Woman' (*C*, III: 262) to a phrase from Schumann's *Faschingsschwank aus Wien* (Carnet 4); and 'the perfumed silkiness' of the impressions conveyed by Vinteuil's music (*C*, III: 381) to a violin passage from Fauré's Piano Quartet No. 1 in C minor (Carnet 3). According to Cahier 55, Franck's *Prelude, Fugue and Variation* provided the origin of the 'virginal' motif of the 'honeysuckle' (*C*, III: 251), and it was the opening of Beethoven's String Quartet No. 12 that inspired 'the charm of certain phrases of Vinteuil's music . . . [a charm which] defies analysis' (*C*, III: 388).

The work of Sybil de Souza, who has concentrated particularly on the sources of the Septet, should also be mentioned. Among many other things, she has pointed out the influence of Franck's cyclic conception of sonata form (1981: 370); but she has also shown the similarity between the theme of the Adagio of Beethoven's Quartet No. 8 and that of the Scherzo of his Quartet No. 12 (1969: 884). For the Septet scoring she cites the precedent of Ravel's *Introduction and Allegro* for flute, clarinet, string quartet and harp (1969: 886), as of Saint-Saëns' Septet for trumpet, string quartet, double bass and piano (1973: 1607, 1980: 202). Painter, similarly, has pointed out the analogy between the description of the Septet and the first movement of Debussy's *La Mer* (1983: 564).

In fact, the game quickly proves fruitless, first because all the evidence suggests that Proust was inspired by a multitude of specific musical data in composing his imaginary works of music, and secondly because, as previous critics have noted (Piroué 1960: 175–7; Matoré and Mecz 1972: 64), his technical descriptions of the little phrase are few and far between, thus leaving the field open to the most diverse interpretations. We must look beyond the little phrase.

Are such investigations of no use whatsoever? There can be no question of rejecting historical perspective *en bloc*, as one might have done twenty years ago; and I should like to define my theoretical position in this regard. Of course Proust was perfectly right to take issue with Sainte-Beuve, inasmuch as the latter's minute piecing together of biographical facts tended to lead to an understanding of the writer rather than of the work. But historical information reassumes its rights if we are prepared to consider the legitimacy of a certain conception of meaning. If, as I believe, the meaning of the text is not only that which is constructed by its reader, but also that which has been invested in it by its author, and if – as the linguist Georges Mounin, following on from the work of Bloomfield (1933), has shown (1969: 255–85) – it is the *placing* [*situation*] of a word, of a phrase, that gives it its meaning, then research into sources and biographical or textual contexts may have a decisive bearing on the *understanding* of a work. While particular references to Saint-Saëns, Franck, Fauré, etc. do not seem to me to illuminate the meaning of the little phrase, or, more exactly, of the passages in Proust concerning music, a knowledge of Proust's poietics, that is, his working methods, is essential in order to determine the relative value of his sources.

As Painter has shown, and as the dedication to Lacretelle confirms, Proust foraged all over the place to create the characters and the imaginary works of art in his novel. Thus a knowledge of any *individual* source cannot contribute much to a better understanding of the book.[9] By the same token, it is hardly possible to discuss the overall structure of *A la recherche* without drawing on the knowledge of the genesis of the novel bequeathed to us by Feuillerat (1934), Bardèche (1971) and all those involved in the new Pléiade edition. When Butor tries to establish, in the purest structuralist spirit, a point-by-point relationship between the number of instruments in the Septet and the number of novels that make up *A la recherche*, he is unable to leave this genesis out of account (1971: 180–5). And when Anne Henry, in her two fine books (1981, 1983), demonstrates what Proust's aesthetics owe to Schelling, Pater and Schopenhauer, and what his analyses of politics, society and language owe to the style of *La Revue des deux mondes*, the sociology of Tarde or the linguistic theories of Max Müller and Michel Bréal, she throws new light on both the meaning and, paradoxically, the originality of Proust's work, for her research reveals the intellectual backdrop against which the writer developed his own ideas. If literary criticism of the past suffered from the fault of relying implicitly on a simplistic mimetic model, the present-day return of historical perspective enables us to define what might be called *a poietic space*, that is to say, the starting-point from which the artist, writer or philosopher develops his own conception of the world, his own ideas, his own style. The poietic space may be compared to the situation created by the position of the pieces in chess: at certain moments of the game this position determines the possibilities of play open to the opponent, while at the same time leaving him a certain freedom of action. In making this point I am not proposing a new method. Let me say merely that I should like to read more frequently, in the field of literary and musical studies, essays as successful as *Wittgenstein's Vienna* by Allan Janik and Stephen Toulmin and *The Intellectual Origins of Leninism* by Alain Besançon.

When Anne Henry writes, 'Vinteuil's score was written by Schopenhauer' (1981: 8), and demonstrates with chapter and verse the decisive influence that *The World as Will and Idea* had on Proust's aesthetics, she must be taken seriously. Besides, did not Proust contrive to give us the 'keys' to his work while at the same time hiding his sources? From *Jean Santeuil* to *A la recherche*, the little phrase passes from Saint-Saëns to Vinteuil, to such effect that *nothing* in the text makes us think of Saint-Saëns. But why, on the other hand, do we have a long disquisition on Wagner, a series of transparent allusions to Debussy's *La Mer* and an explicit reference to Beethoven's late quartets? We have to leave the text and pursue instead what it suggests, and it is on this aspect of Proust's poietics that we shall concentrate.

If our definition of poietic space – whether philosophical or musical – signifies a return to history, and if a return to history characterises the very period in which we live, then this return is something that has taken place *since* the emergence of structuralism. Without going into detail, we can say that one of the historic merits of structuralism, following on from the narrowly biographical approaches typical of earlier literary criticism, has been to bring about a return to the text. It is one of the fundamental hypotheses of this essay that the role played by music in Proust's novel cannot adequately be interpreted without an examination of the themes that intersect in each 'musical' passage. Such an examination should be not only as exhaustive as possible but also successive, that is to say, it should take into account the order in which these themes appear in the course of *A la recherche*.

It is well known that there are three imaginary creative artists in the work of Proust: the writer Bergotte, the painter Elstir and the composer Vinteuil. However, little is known about the work of the first; as for the second, Proust gives a superb description of *Carquethuit Harbour*, yet the work of Elstir as such appears (apart from numerous allusions) only once. On the other hand, the works of Vinteuil – his Sonata and Septet – go right through *A la recherche*, inspiring several big 'set pieces' as well as some fragmentary allusions[10] to which I shall refer where appropriate. The set pieces are as follows:

1 The 'archetypal' performance and the Andante at the Verdurins' (*S*, I: 224–34).
2 Other Verdurin performances (*ibid*.: 238–9).
3 The Sonata played on the piano by Odette (*ibid*.: 258–60).
4 The Sonata played on the piano at the Verdurins' (*ibid*.: 288); the little phrase on the outskirts of Paris (*ibid*.: 295).
5 The Sonata played on piano and violin at the Saint-Euverte soirée (*ibid*.: 375–84).
6 The 'transmission' of the Sonata to the Narrator by Odette (*WBG*, I: 570–5).
7 The comparison of Vinteuil with Wagner (*C*, III: 154–9).
8 The Septet (*ibid*.: 250–65).
9 The sessions on the pianola (*ibid*.: 378–90).

Of itself this simple list determines the content and method of the present study.

The works of Vinteuil mark out the psychological evolution of the characters, as in the amorous relationship of Swann and Odette or in that of the Narrator and Albertine. Consequently they act as milestones in the Narrator's discovery of his vocation as a writer, of the nature of the 'true life' and of the recovery of Time through the literary work. The present essay is explicitly intended as a sequel to the article 'La Construction musicale de la *Recherche du temps perdu*' by Pierre Costil (1958–9), who seems to have been the first to establish beyond doubt the essential role played by the Sonata and the Septet in the work's structure: it is the Narrator's meditation on the nature of music that leads him to see in it the ideal model for literature and to decide to devote his life to literary work. The Vinteuil Septet inspires a veritable revelation: 'Proust's novel', writes Costil, 'is a *quest**[11] for the true reality beyond what is perceptible' (1959: 102).

To my mind there is only one possible method for analysing the role played by music in the novel: it consists of examining, one after the other, each of the passages relating to Vinteuil's works. This is what Matoré and Mecz do, with fine judgment and skill, in *Musique et structure romanesque dans la 'Recherche du temps perdu'* (1972). Yet while they rightly insist upon the role played by Vinteuil's works in the progress of the Narrator towards his vocation, they make, surprisingly, no reference whatever to the analysis of Costil. Perhaps it is for this reason that this painstaking and comprehensive study of the themes that intermingle in the musical passages of *A la recherche* does not succeed in conveying the profound teleology of each individual element, that irresistible heartbeat which culminates in revelation and which is based, as I shall try to show, on a fundamental progression articulated in three stages − being as much a characteristic of Proust's perception as it is of his aesthetics and metaphysics. Moreover, the authors omit (1972: 162–80) to comment on the passage where Proust compares musical and verbal language (*C*, III: 260). This is, in my view, the key moment of the novel, as Benoist-Méchin observed as long ago as 1926 (1957: 135), even if he makes no reference to Proust's homosexuality and does not dwell on the connection between Vinteuil's music and the structure of the book.

I cannot therefore subscribe to the basic conclusion of Matoré and Mecz, namely that 'the relationship between Vinteuil's music and the problem of vocation, established by a certain number of encounters of the Narrator with the musician's work, nevertheless remains *gratuitous*. Nothing, in fact, predestined this art to promote a literary vocation' (1972: 280). Or again: 'The writer regards the musical work as a *pretext*' (1972: 158).

In order to understand the role played by music in relation to literary vocation, one must take seriously Proust's explicit references to Wagner, Debussy, Beethoven and Schopenhauer and consider them in their order of appearance; in other words, one must determine the role they play at each stage of the quest. It is because he considers the three

---

* Costil uses the old French spelling, *queste*, rather than the more usual *quête*. [Trans.]

musicians in chronological order and not according to their function in the novel, and because he makes only two brief allusions to Schopenhauer, that Piroué is able to assert – even though he, too, recognises the fundamental role played by music in the Narrator's journey towards his vocation (1960: 7, 86, 108) – that Proust 'has missed his rendezvous with music itself' (*ibid.*: 60); he also asserts, with regard to Beethoven, that 'Proust remains on this side of music, on the side where music is still mixed up with every kind of emotion' (*ibid.*: 165), and that 'of a music which satisfies us, Proust has retained only the moments when we are racked with dissatisfaction' (*ibid.*: 104). On the contrary, I shall show how the Narrator makes a journey which, in leading him from Debussy to Beethoven, enables him to discover in music the embodiment of that art which, according to Schopenhauer, can 'arrest the wheel of time' and consequently guide him to his literary vocation and the 'true life'.

I would find it difficult to talk about the '*anecdotal* character that is assumed by the music associated with the principal events of *A la recherche*' (Matoré and Mecz 1972: 288). On the ground that Proust was not a professional musician, and perhaps also because when discussing music he does not draw on the technical concepts of music theory, writers have tended to underestimate the extent of his musical *understanding*. In particular, the relevance of a *perceptual* approach to music has been dismissed – as if music could only be discussed when 'perceived and analysed objectively [?]'* (Piroué 1960: 136), and as if it were of secondary importance to consider music in terms of the various effects it produces and the varied ideas it awakes. These criticisms do not in the least detract from the value of my predecessors' work, and a perusal of their writings cannot be too highly recommended. But because their generally negative verdict seems to be tied to a somewhat restricted concept of music, which is belied both by recent developments in musicology and by changes in the way people think, I have felt it necessary to rehabilitate *Proust as musician* – if that epithet may be used in the first sense given in the French *Robert* dictionary, i.e. 'someone who is capable of appreciating music'.

The musical texts in *A la recherche* occupy a relatively small number of pages. Consequently I shall inevitably fall back on examples already

* Nattiez's [?]. [Trans.]

quoted or discussed by others. But I believe that there is room for new light to be shed upon Proust's relation to music, if one but considers it from the perspective of the influence that music may exert on a writer. That is, at any rate, my hypothesis.

2

Parsifal as redemptive model for the redemptive work

In *The Captive* there is a passage which is quite extraordinary, not only because of its immense beauty but also because it is the only place in the whole of *A la recherche* where the Vinteuil Sonata is explicitly compared to a real work. 'Comparison' here must be taken to mean not only the artistic analogy that Proust wishes to stress but also the physical proximity through which he makes it manifest:

Could life console me for the loss of art? Was there in art a more profound reality, in which our true personality finds an expression that is not afforded it by the activities of life? For every great artist seems so different from all the rest, and gives us so strongly that sensation of individuality for which we seek in vain in our everyday existence! Just as I was thinking thus, I was struck by a passage in the sonata. It was a passage with which I was quite familiar, but sometimes our attention throws a different light upon things which we have known for a long time and we remark in them what we have never seen before. As I played the passage, and although Vinteuil had been trying to express in it a fancy which would have been wholly foreign to Wagner, I could not help murmuring '*Tristan*,' with the smile of an old family friend discovering a trace of the grandfather in an intonation, a gesture of the grandson who has never set eyes on him. And as the friend then examines a photograph which enables him to specify the likeness, so, on top of Vinteuil's sonata, I set up on the music-rest the score of *Tristan*, a selection from which was being given that afternoon, as it happened, at a Lamoureux concert.   (*C*, III: 155)

Thus the affiliation between Wagner and Vinteuil − affiliation in the literal, genealogical sense − is expressly established. And while in the text of *A la recherche*, as we shall see below, Proust takes the imaginary works of Vinteuil as a starting-point for his reflections on music − so that in this instance the Sonata serves only as a pretext for introducing Wagner — at the same time the allusion to Wagner clarifies the function of Vinteuil's little phrase.

Proust begins by evoking the Wagnerian technique of the leitmotif. One immediately thinks of *A la recherche* itself when he writes:

> I was struck by how much reality there is in the work of Wagner as I contemplated once more those insistent, fleeting themes which visit an act, recede only to return again and again, and, sometimes distant, drowsy, almost detached, are at other moments, while remaining vague, so pressing and so close, so internal, so organic, so visceral, that they seem like the reprise not so much of a musical motif as of an attack of neuralgia.   (*C*, III: 156)

This train of thought leads back to the theme that suggested the Wagner–Vinteuil comparison: the search for individuality. The Narrator has found it not in life but in art, in music and most particularly in Wagner, because behind each work there lies the originality of a particular creative artist and because the work of art itself aims to 'combin[e] diverse individualities'. Referring to Wagner, Proust describes the means by which music calls on particular configurations of sound to depict each particular appearance of a character or of an identical idea: 'Even that which, in this music, is most independent of the emotion that it arouses in us preserves its outward and absolutely precise reality; the song of a bird, the ring of a hunter's horn, the air that a shepherd plays upon his pipe, each carves its silhouette of sound against the horizon' (*C*, III: 156–7). The allusions are quite clear: the bird in *Siegfried*; Siegfried's horn, or more probably the hunters' in *Tannhäuser*, or perhaps those at the beginning of the second act of *Tristan*; and, without any doubt, the shepherd's lament played on the cor anglais in *Tristan* Act III. Since the whole passage under consideration is based on an analogy with *Tristan*, it will be useful to examine this last reference in detail, and so provide the first example in this study of the advantage that may be derived from an analysis of Proustian allusions. This pipe-tune is perhaps the only leitmotif in all of Wagner's works on which we have a commentary by a character in the opera itself. It will be useful, then, to refer to the libretto.

Tristan addresses the theme:

> Am I thus to understand
> that sad old tune

with its plaintive sound?
On the evening breeze
it sent its lament
when once to a child
it announced his father's death;
through morning's grey,
more fearful yet,
where the son
learnt of his mother's fate.
He begot me and died;
she, dying, gave me birth.
To them too
must have wailed
the old tune's
mournful plaint
that once asked me,
and asks me now
to what fate I was destined
when I was born?
To what fate?
the old tune
tells me again: –
to yearn and die!
No! Ah no!
It is not so!
To yearn, to yearn!
Dying, still to yearn,
not of yearning to die!
What never dies
now calls, yearning,
to the distant physician
for the peace of death.

(Wagner 1981: 43–4)

Noteworthy here is the fact that the tune played by the shepherd has taken on different meanings in the course of Tristan's life. After having been associated with the tragic circumstances of his birth, it now foretells his future. But is this really the correct interpretation? Thus Wagner himself, criticising in advance all those makers of leitmotif Michelin Guides, emphasises the leitmotif's semantic flexibility. Proust, who must surely have known the libretto of *Tristan*, available in Paris ever since Wagner published his *Four Dramatic Poems* at the time of the first Paris performance of *Tannhäuser*, cannot have been oblivious to what might equally well have been said about Swann's little phrase: a few notes of variable significance, to which Swann attributes a different meaning every time his feelings change. A language, certainly, but a fickle one.

Proust's thoughts then rise to a higher, more general plane. The great works of the nineteenth century, he says, are all incomplete. For him, Balzac with *La Comédie humaine*, Hugo with *La Légende des siècles* and Michelet with *La Bible de l'humanité* gave to their individual works, retrospectively, a unity which their authors had not at first imagined. The digression via literature is only incidental. Proust brings us back to Wagner:

> The other musician, he who was delighting me at this moment, Wagner, retrieving some exquisite fragment from a drawer of his writing-table to introduce it, as a retrospectively necessary theme, into a work he had not even thought of at the time he composed it, then having composed a first mythological opera, and a second, and afterwards others still, and perceiving all of a sudden that he had written a tetralogy,[1] must have felt something of the same exhilaration as Balzac when the latter . . . suddenly decided . . . that [his books] would be better brought together in a cycle in which the same characters would reappear.   (*C*, III: 157–8)

Later he gives a specific example of the integration into a work of a melody drawn from the memory: displaying the same 'Vulcan-like skill' that he acknowledges in Wagner, Proust combines the joy that is evoked by the shepherd's tune played on the cor anglais at the moment when Isolde arrives with the joy he believes Wagner felt 'when he discovered in his memory the shepherd's tune, incorporated it into his work, [and] gave it its full wealth of meaning' (*C*, III: 158). 'Before the great orchestral movement that precedes the return of Isolde, it is the work itself that has attracted towards itself the half-forgotten air of a shepherd's pipe' (*ibid.*).[2]

Vigneron has shown just how perfectly mythical Proust's description of the poietics of Balzac, Hugo, Michelet and Wagner may be: 'In describing the genesis of *The Ring* and of *La Comédie humaine* in such an inaccurate fashion, is he not trying implicitly to explain and justify, through the use of illustrious precedents, the way in which he himself expanded *A la recherche du temps perdu*?' (1946: 380). No doubt

Vigneron is right, but, staying within my own domain, I think it important to show how Proust's allusions to the history of *The Ring* or to Wagner's working methods may help us to understand his relationship to music.

In the first place, it is precisely correct that the famous cor anglais solo which is heard just after the curtain goes up on the third act of *Tristan*, and which later returns, as Proust indicates, in accordance with the events of the drama, has risen up out of the composer's memory. Indeed, it was inspired by a Venetian gondolier's song, as Wagner himself writes in his autobiography, *My Life*:

On a sleepless night that drove me out on the balcony of my apartment at about three o'clock in the morning, I heard for the first time the famous old folksong of the gondolieri. I thought the first call, piercing the stillness of the night like a harsh lament, emanated from the Rialto, barely a quarter hour's distance away, or thereabouts; from a similar distance this would be answered from another quarter in the same way. This strange melancholy dialogue . . . was repeated frequently at longish intervals. . . . Such were the impressions that seemed most characteristic of Venice to me during my stay, and they remained with me until the completion of the second act of *Tristan*, and perhaps even helped to inspire the long-drawn-out lament for the shepherd's horn at the beginning of the third act.   (1983: 578)

The situation described by Wagner corresponds precisely to what Proust wishes to evoke: the gondoliers' songs have nothing to do with Tristan and Isolde, but it is by transfiguring them for his opera that the composer gives them the specific meaning that we find in them today.

The genesis of *The Ring* as seen by Proust is treated in a summary fashion which is the novelist's licence. It is well known, of course, that Wagner began by writing the libretto for *Götterdämmerung* (under the title *Siegfrieds Tod*); he then started setting it to music (in August 1850), but gave up and instead wrote the libretto for *Siegfried*; finally, having decided to commit himself to a tetralogy, he went back to *Das Rheingold* before finishing with *Die Walküre*. It was only afterwards that he composed the music. Proust's 'all of a sudden' is a little excessive, to say the least. By the same token, Wagner was not a 'bottom-drawer composer' who wrote fragments independently of the works in which they were to be inserted. Proust is here thinking specifically of the 'Good Friday Spell', as the following passage from *Contre Sainte-Beuve* shows:

Wagner had composed the 'Good Friday Spell' before he thought of writing *Parsifal*, and put it into the opera later on. But the additions . . ., these lovely things that are brought in, the new relationships suddenly perceived by his genius between separated parts of his work, which rejoin each other, come to life, are henceforth inseparable, are they not his finest creative intuitions?

(*CSB*: 274)*

Now, the *Voyage artistique à Bayreuth* by Albert Lavignac, that great classic of French Wagnerism which appeared in 1897, contains the following note on the subject of the 'Spell': 'It had been written a long time before the rest of the score' (1905: 498). Several reasons converge to suggest that we have here the source of Proust's information.

First, given the Wagnerian atmosphere at the turn of the century which includes Proust among its leading figures, he could hardly have remained ignorant of this 'best seller', which was already in its fifty-seventh impression as early as 1903. Above all, however, it seems clear that Lavignac's information is false: we can search through the biographies of Glasenapp, Ellis and Newman – not to mention the more recent works of Gutman, von Westernhagen and Gregor-Dellin – without finding any mention of the 'Good Friday Spell' having been written before the composition of *Parsifal*. This is confirmed by the *Wagner Werk-Verzeichnis* (Deathridge, Geck and Voss 1986: 550–2). Further research is necessary to establish the source of Lavignac's error. Was he confused by Wagner's statement in *My Life* that he had drafted the libretto of *Parsifal* on 10 April 1857 (twenty years, indeed, before he began writing it in earnest), under the spell of a Good Friday?[3] Or was Lavignac confused by the fact that Wagner invented the theme of the Flower Maidens on 9 February 1876, at the time when he was composing the *March for the Centenary of American Independence*, whereas he did not begin to compose the music of *Parsifal* until August 1877? What matters here is that Lavignac, by the very fact of his error, seems to be the only possible source of Proust's information; and if I dwell on this point it is because the *Voyage artistique à Bayreuth* will prove useful later – though in connection with Beethoven.

It is not surprising, in any case, that Proust should have been struck by a note in Lavignac concerning a passage in Wagner to which he often refers. We have seen one explicit mention of it in the dedication

---

* Translation adapted from *By Way of Sainte-Beuve*, trans. Sylvia Townsend Warner (London: Hogarth Press, 1984), p. 136. [Trans.]

to Jacques de Lacretelle, and it returns frequently in Proust's life and work. Biographers have recounted the episode in the castle of Coucy, where Proust sang the 'Good Friday Spell' in company with Fénelon (Painter 1983: 286). It would not seem superfluous to quote the following passage: 'It was enough . . . [that the] snow-balls . . . should remind me that the Good Friday music in *Parsifal* symbolises a natural miracle which one could see performed every year if one had the sense to look for it' (*WBG*, I: 683); or the passage in which M. de Charlus says of a Jewish banker at a concert: 'He soon recovered his habitually blissful expression when he heard the Good Friday music' (*CP*, II: 1142). We shall see presently how this very same music played a particularly important role in the genesis of *A la recherche*.

In short – and this is the crucial point – what Lavignac says, even if his facts are wrong, corresponds too closely to Proust's own poietic processes to be ignored.

It is well known that Proust worked painstakingly at a particular passage, and so embarked upon digressions, those famous 'paperoles' which make the study of his manuscripts so difficult. In the words of Bardèche, Proust constructed 'panels' (1971, II: 94) and then proceeded to put them together in a 'montage' (*ibid.*: 164). This was how the Venice episode, conceived and written at the very beginning of Proust's work on *A la recherche*, finally found its place in *The Captive* (*ibid.*: 217). The grandmother's death was supposed to occur during the holiday in Venice but was inserted in *The Fugitive* (*ibid.*: 197); the episode of the uneven paving-stones was written before that of the madeleine (1971, I: 170–1); and so on. What Lavignac says of the 'Spell' corresponds exactly to Proust's manner of working – one might almost say, his poietic style. Montage would be created through transference and even through suppression. Bardèche reports the disappearance of an entire panel describing, specifically, 'The Good Friday Spell' (1971, II: 279). We shall come back to this. In short, the predilection for symmetrical constructions and balance between the parts that is clearly apparent in the original plan of *A la recherche* – this desire for *closure* in the work – is countered by a tendency towards expansion, not only in the composition of phrases and paragraphs but also in the large-scale design of the novel.

At this point it may be useful to give a general summary of the genesis of the work as a whole, some knowledge of which is in any case necessary for an understanding of what follows.

By way of introduction, there is what might be called the pre-*Recherche*, which corresponds to the project of *Contre Sainte-Beuve* (1908–9). This is a theoretical work, but one in which some fictional episodes already appear: bedtime at Combray, the two ways, the poetry of names, the stay at Balbec, the meeting of the girls. With the madeleine and the paving-stones, Proust holds at once the beginning and the end of his future novel (though nothing is worked out fully), as well as certain elements of his conception of literature. But the novel-form soon competes with the essay. From this same period survive rough drafts of the stay at Balbec, the description of Venice, the marriages of Saint-Loup and Jupien; and shortly afterwards Proust abandons the theoretical essay, for it has provided him with the epilogue of his novel. This is on 27 November 1909.

The genesis of *A la recherche* will itself pass through four phases.

First of all, the project of *The Intermittencies of the Heart*, planned in two volumes: 'Time Lost' and 'Time Regained'. 'Time Lost' was to be divided into three parts: *Combray*, consisting of four chapters (the mother's kiss; the madeleine, Combray and Aunt Léonie; Sunday in Combray; the two ways), *Swann in Love* and a third part which corresponds to the end of the present first volume and the first half of *Within a Budding Grove* and which is itself divided into three chapters: 'Place-names: the name', 'Madame Swann at home' and 'Place-names: the place' (up to the end of the first stay at Balbec – I: 845).

The desire for symmetry and balance is clearly evident in this initial plan: the two volumes, the three parts with 'Swann in love' at the centre, and a third part constructed on the same principle, with the place-names framing Mme Swann just as the 'Combray' section and the section on the Guermantes Way frame 'Swann in love'. As for *Time Regained*, in the 1910–11 version (Cahiers 58 and 57 have been published by Henri Bonnet under the title *Matinée chez la Princesse de Guermantes*) it was supposed to consist of two parts: 'Perpetual adoration' and 'The ball of the heads'.

The publication of the present *Swann's Way* in 1913 by Grasset corresponds to the beginning of a second phase. It is at this time that the present general title, *A la recherche du temps perdu*, emerges. Unlike the *Intermittencies of the Heart* project, the first volume stops after 'Place-names: the name', this solely for technical reasons: Grasset had asked Proust to keep the end of *Swann's Way* aside for a second volume, which

was to be called *The Guermantes Way*. It is announced for 1914 on the
back of the 1913 volume containing the two chapters already mentioned (which will make up the first part of *Within a Budding Grove*):
'Madame Swann at home' and 'Place-names: the place'. But already the
novel begins to proliferate by way of the Guermantes: 'First glimpses
of the Baron de Charlus and of Robert de Saint-Loup', 'Names of
people: the Duchesse de Guermantes', 'The salon of Madame de
Villeparisis' (cf. Part I of the present *Guermantes Way*). The same
cover page also announces the contents of *Time Regained*: 'Within a
budding grove', 'The Princesse de Guermantes', 'M. de Charlus and
the Verdurins', 'The death of my grandmother', 'The intermittencies
of the heart', 'The vices and virtues of Padua and Combray', 'Madame
de Cambremer', 'The marriage of Robert de Saint-Loup', 'Perpetual
adoration'.

Thus, as Bardèche has so rightly observed, *Within a Budding Grove*
never existed in the original plan as a project in its own right. Nor did
Albertine. Grasset possesses *The Guermantes Way* from its beginning
to the end of Part I, and Proust has already written a first version of
the present *Time Regained*. Some episodes also of *Cities of the Plain* survive in the rough drafts of 1909–10.

But the great work goes through a third phase: even if the character
Albertine is prefigured as early as 1909–10 (Tadié 1987: lviii), it seems
that the love affair of Proust and Agostinelli (1914–15) triggers off a
new expansion of the novel. As a result, the episode of the 'blossoming
girls', which has been present in Proust's mind from the start (cf. the
contents of *Contre Sainte-Beuve*), grows in size: by leaving Grasset for
Gallimard, Proust can now make *Within a Budding Grove* a book in its
own right. When, delayed by the war, it appears on 30 November
1918, the whole project consists of five volumes: Proust announces that
The Guermantes Way is to be followed by *Cities of the Plain* Part I and
a fifth volume, *Cities of the Plain* Part II (*Time Regained*), in which *The
Captive* and *The Fugitive* are no more than chapters. The introduction
of the character Albertine, together with all the new expansions that
Proust expects to incorporate in the last three volumes announced in
1919, allows us to speak of a *second A la recherche*, grafted onto the
original plan (and to be drafted in its entirety, from *Cities of the Plain*
to *Time Regained*, in 1914–18).

Between 1919 and 1922, however, the composition of the relationship with Albertine will assume such an importance that *A la recherche* goes through a final phase (Tadié 1987: lxxxix-xc). In 1920 Proust has the idea of linking *The Guermantes Way* Part II with *Cities* Part I, which would still give us a novel in five volumes. But in 0922 he is talking of a *Cities of the Plain* Part III (*The Captive*) and a *Cities of the Plain* Part IV (*The Fugitive*), proposing to bring them together under the title *Cities of the Plain* Part III (Sections 1 and 2). Given the length that these episodes have already assumed, we now have a novel in six or seven volumes.

Like the genesis of *A la recherche*, the poietics of Wagner are better known to us today than they could have been for Proust. We can attempt, therefore, to look beyond the differences between the two artists – the absence of displaced panels in Wagner – for deeper connections. We have seen how the episodes of the madeleine and of the paving-stones, which are separated by almost three thousand pages in the final version, appear next to one another in *Contre Sainte-Beuve*. This is the exact text:

When under our foot a paving-stone in a courtyard can awaken just one of those sensations that we had experienced on treading on the paving in the Baptistery of St Mark's, when the taste of a madeleine soaked in tea can bring a piece of the past close to us without even allowing us to retrace it, we perceive, overwhelmed by an irresistible joy and charm, the degree to which the real past – even the most humble – differs from that which the memory of the intellect presents to us when it is summoned up by the will (Esquisse XIV, in *NE*, I: 701).

Similarly, Wagner scrawled a musical sketch for the beginning of *Siegfrieds Tod*, which was the first version of *Götterdämmerung*, in August 1850. In that same sketch we find the wave-like figures that open *Das Rheingold*, with its obsession with E flat (the very start of *The Ring*), the motif of Wotan's spear (*Das Rheingold*, Scene 2), the motif of the *Todesverkündigung* (*Die Walküre*, Act II), the 'Ride of the Valkyries' (Act III), the theme of Brünnhilde's 'justification' (Act III), some features of the scene in *Siegfried* in which Mime thinks of Fafner (*Siegfried*, Act I), Siegfried's motif of jubilation (Act I) and an anticipation of the song of the Norns (Prologue to *Götterdämmerung*);[4] these elements appear at all conceivable points in the present tetralogy. In both cases we are in the presence of what Bardèche has called a 'nebula' (1971, II: 23), that is, the condensation, at a specific point in the text and in the creative process, of a series of themes and ideas which will later 'explode', scattering to the four corners of the finished work. And just as Wagner 'went back' from the libretto of *Götterdämmerung* to that of *Das Rheingold*, so Proust went back from the episode of the paving-stones, written first, to that of the madeleine.

Wagner's poietics, then, are not exactly comparable to those of Proust, but both artists were haunted by an obsession with unity. To use Piroué's apt phrase, Proust posthumously regarded Wagner as a 'professional friend' (1960: 107). The search for unity generates a 'single work'. If, unlike Proust, Wagner was prevented by the constraints of opera from writing only *one* work, nevertheless *The Ring*, with its four operas composed over a period of twenty-six years, constitutes an analogous project which remains unique in the history of music. The chronology of Wagner's creative life shows how closely his projects were bound up with one another. Wagner thought about his works for a long time before he actually wrote them: we know today that he made the first sketch for *Die Meistersinger* (composed in 1861–3) as early as July 1845, shortly after *Tannhäuser*, and that he may already have been thinking of the subjects of *Tristan* and *Parsifal* (composed in 1857–9 and 1877–82 respectively) in his Dresden period (1843–9). One has only to glance at the chronology of *The Ring* to see the extent to which the composition of *Die Meistersinger* was intertwined with that of *Siegfried* and *Götterdämmerung* (see Nattiez 1983: 272–3).

It is not surprising, then, to find echoes of one work in another. Lohengrin is the son of Parsifal; in an early version of *Tristan*, Parsifal came to his sickbed in Act III; Hans Sachs, in *Die Meistersinger*, evokes the sorrow of King Mark, complete with a musical quotation from *Tristan*; a passage in *Die Meistersinger* takes up the music of *Siegfried*; and one can read in Cosima Wagner's diary that disenchanted remark concerning the third act of *Götterdämmerung*, 'Here I might as well just write: "See *Tristan*, Act III" '. Proust could easily cite the example of Wagner's libretti when he speaks to Albertine of novelists who are constantly rewriting the same book. From *Der fliegende Holländer* to *Parsifal*, with the possible exception of *Die Meistersinger*, the scenario is the same: that of a female redeemer – Senta, Elisabeth, Elsa, Isolde, Brünnhilde, Kundry – who sacrifices herself to save the man. Like Proust, yes, but in a different way, Wagner wrote only one work. There is indeed in Wagner that same passion for completeness which expresses itself through deleted waverings, through reminiscences of one work in another and through his truly Proustian obsession with the single work which manages to incorporate all the others. *The Ring* is his answer to that ambition.

The desire for unity, for unification, manifests itself in other aspects of the work too. We know that Proust vacillated between a theoretical essay (*Contre Sainte-Beuve*) and a fictional work, to the point where the final revelation opens the way to an aesthetic theory. The chronology of *The Ring* shows clearly how the idea for that work occurred to Wagner in conjunction with a theoretical project which he realised in his essays *Art and Revolution, The Art Work of the Future* and *Opera and Drama*, written while the libretto was going through a period of gestation – a conjunction so close, as I will show elsewhere,[5] that it is quite possible to see the plot of *The Ring* as an allegorical transposition of the composer's theoretical concerns.

In each case the expansion of the work by an author in search of unity leads to a duality in its characters. Wagner, beginning the composition of *The Ring* with *Siegfrieds Tod*, the first version of *Götterdämmerung*, was at first interested in the character Siegfried; then, when he 'went back' to *Das Rheingold*, he gave a greater importance to Wotan than he had done before. As Chomskians would say, Wagner carries out expansion to the left. Proust, by contrast, proceeds by expanding to the right: by comparison with the first *A la recherche*, where the Narrator takes an interest first in Gilberte and then in Mme de Guermantes, the introduction of the character Albertine, together with all the new episodes of *Within a Budding Grove* and *The Fugitive*, creates the imbalance already mentioned. *The Ring* suffers from an identical problem: even though the four days that pass between the theft of the ring from the Rhine and its recovery end with a return to a state of nature, the centre of gravity has shifted from Siegfried to Wotan. And if these displacements provide riddles of exegesis for the reader and critic of *A la recherche*, those of *The Ring* pose real interpretative problems for the theatrical producer (see Nattiez 1983, Part I).

In both works, again, characters appear as doubles for one another. Alberich is the evil double of Wotan, but Brünnhilde is Wotan's feminine double and Siegmund the successful double of Siegfried.[6] In *A la recherche*, Venice is the double of Combray, Charlus the double of Swann and Swann the double of the Narrator.

The search for unity is also the obsession of the *Gesamtkunstwerk*. If Wagner's explicit intention in his operas (see *The Art Work of the Future*) was to integrate not only poetry, music and dance but also painting, sculpture and architecture, *A la recherche* corresponds to a similar venture, in which architecture, painting, literature and music contribute major elements to the work's fabric, with the essential role being assigned to music, as I shall show in detail in chapter 3. It is worth pointing out that Proust must certainly have known the summary of Wagner's theoretical ideas provided by Baudelaire in his *Richard Wagner et le Tannhäuser à Paris* (Piroué 1960: 113), if not indeed Wagner's own 'Letter to Villot Concerning Music', which the composer used as a preface to his *Four Dramatic Poems*.

In both cases the attempt to construct self-contained quasi-worlds has produced the same reaction: the proliferation of those 'minutiae' in Wagner's score which exasperated Nietzsche but are the delight of a Boulez; a similar proliferation of psychological and descriptive detail in Proust. To prevent a scattered effect, and to give these pieces of marquetry work their unity, some guiding thread is necessary: the leitmotif in one case, a system of preparations and anticipations in the other. The whole thing flowing in a wave that nothing really checks: the cadences at the end of Wagner's acts are but temporary suspensions of the 'endless melody'; while Proust's chapter divisions are often artificial, as are, moreover, the divisions between volumes over which he took so little trouble, such as that between *Swann's Way* and *Within a Budding Grove*, which he did not attempt to correct, or the transition from *The Fugitive* to *Time Regained*, which does not seem to be indicated in the manuscript and is still a subject of controversy (see Tadié 1987: xc).

It was only because one cannot prolong an opera beyond a certain number of hours that Wagner managed to stop. The writer knows no such constraints (on this topic, see Piroué 1960: 115). But since *The Ring* and *A la recherche* both cost their authors more than twenty years' work, it is not surprising that they offer little of the stylistic unity their authors would have wished. Boulez has observed that as *The Ring* unfolds, from *Das Rheingold* to *Götterdämmerung*, we can read in it the history of Wagner's musical language (1986: 263–4). It bespeaks no lack of admiration for Proust if we remark a difference of literary style which distinguishes *Cities of the Plain*, *The Captive* and *The Fugitive* from the works that precede them. With *Time Regained* we find ourselves back in the stylistic atmosphere of the first two volumes. Works like *The Ring* and *A la recherche* try to annul the passing of Time; and this is how Time takes its revenge on works that seek to escape from it.

Like the characters of *A la recherche*, Proust's book and *The Ring* are affected by Time. When Proust describes certain nineteenth-century works as unfinished, he is probably haunted by the idea of not finishing his own; and it is certainly with a hint of envy that he meditates on the completion of *The Ring*. It is not surprising, then, that the two artists should display a similar attitude with regard to time, the same fear of time. That of Proust needs no comment. That of Wagner is perhaps less well known: like the novelist, the composer was obsessed with the idea of finishing his work so that he could contemplate it during his lifetime. 'Vollendet das ewige Werk' – 'completed, the eternal work' – says Wotan, standing before Valhalla (*Das Rheingold*, Scene 2). And one month before his death Wagner was thinking that he still owed the world a *Tannhäuser*: he hoped he would have time to revise it once more. Is it not symptomatic that his favourite scene in *The Ring* was that of the Norns, where past, present and future conjoin at a fixed point in Time? He would often play it to himself on the piano. To write a work which tells of the birth and death of the world, and which recaptures the original state of nature, is to attempt to conjure up eternity in a few hours of music.

We can understand, then, why Wagner's work should have represented for Proust an exemplary model of the complete work that was to be created, one which respected the individuality of the characters and motifs but transcended and integrated them in the unity. The complete work, in other words not only *A la recherche* itself, which may be sensed behind every phrase that Proust wrote about Wagner, but also, and above all, the *imaginary* work that the Narrator will resolve to write (even if, on reading the novel a second time, we believe this 'imaginary' work to be the one we are reading). Consequently we should not be surprised if it was in Wagner – as I shall now try to show – that Proust found the model for the fundamental subject of *A la recherche*: the quest for the absolute through the medium of the work of art.

I said at the outset that the article of Pierre Costil, 'La Construction musicale de la *Recherche du temps perdu*', seemed to have established the place of music in the overall structure of *A la recherche* beyond any doubt. Indeed, '*The final revelation, inspired by music,*[7] brings into harmonious synthesis, in order to elucidate them, the poetic impressions which [Proust] had amassed since childhood, and which had stayed alive in his memory like so many incitements to the search for true reality' (1958: 471). Costil's analysis takes as its starting-point a debate about both the construction and the poietics of the novel. The author, in effect, takes issue with Feuillerat's opinion that the 'second *Recherche*' is less well constructed than the first. Basing his case on a draft published in the *Figaro littéraire* of 13 November 1946 – a draft which, he proves, corresponds to the scene in *Within a Budding Grove* in which Odette 'transmits' the Vinteuil Sonata to the Narrator, and not, as the newspaper introduction claims, to the Saint-Euverte performance – Costil demonstrates that the various appearances of Vinteuil's works throughout *A la recherche* constitute the essential axis of the novel in its final state. On the one hand, the descriptions of the musical works are closely bound up with passion, time and memory (1958: 494), that is, with the essential themes of *A la recherche*. On the other hand, the Sonata corresponds to the failed quest of Swann, that of the amateur, whereas the Septet, by contrast, enables the Narrator to grasp 'the essence of happiness' and 'the certainty of the realities *revealed* by art, that certainty which is the guarantee of the work to which he devotes himself with all his being' (1958: 486–7): this is the path of the artist. 'Reliving Swann's experience, but this time taking it to its conclusion, he will be brought by his love to a comprehension of the truths that music has disclosed to him' (1959: 100). Thus, says Costil, the 'transmission' scene 'was specially composed by Proust with an eye to the final arrangement of *A la recherche*' (1958: 476). The whole work, he continues, 'is in its way a modern *Queste du Saint-Graal*' (1958: 486). Costil does not know how right he is.

Indeed, I should like to demonstrate the role played by Wagner's *Parsifal* in the genesis of *A la recherche* and the way in which a knowledge of this role helps us to a better understanding of the function of music in the novel.

In the first *A la recherche*, that of the 1913 plan, the music of Vinteuil is represented solely by the Sonata in *Swann's Way*. Although one can only endorse the idea that the 'transmission' scene was added later in

order to create a link with the Septet episode in *The Captive* and so provide an opportunity for the Narrator to take up the quest where Swann
left off, I find it hard to go along with Costil when he asserts that,
'while [Proust] had already had recourse to music in order to write
"Swann in love", he had not yet envisaged a musical structure
extending over the whole novel' (1959: 108).

We were already aware, thanks to the information supplied by
Bardèche (which Costil could not have known in 1958), that the
manuscript of *Time Regained* included a 'panel' devoted to the 'Good
Friday Spell'. But before the publication of the *Matinée chez la
Princesse de Guermantes*, edited by Henri Bonnet, it was impossible to
recognise the full importance of the role played by this passage in the
organisation of the first *A la recherche*.

It is 1910–11. Proust has written his final chapter, which is to be
entitled 'Matinée chez la Princesse de Guermantes' ('Reception at the
Princesse de Guermantes' house') and divided into two parts:
'Perpetual adoration' and 'The ball of the heads' (Bonnet 1982, in
MPG: 15). Now, what do we find there?

The chapter begins with a clear statement of the reason for the
reception:

I had arrived a few days earlier in Paris, where my doctors had, at last, just
permitted me to make my home – something long denied me. My mother told
me that my aunt, my grandmother's sister, who had come up from the country
for a few days, had been to see her and had told her that the first Paris performance of the second act of *Parsifal* would be taking place two days later at
the Princesse de Guermantes'.   (*MPG*: 114)

In fact it is the third act, as Bonnet points out (*ibid.*: 172), since the
passage that is to be played and described is the 'Good Friday Spell'.
As in the *Time Regained* that we know, the Narrator consults the books
in the library: 'I was very pleased to be shut in for the duration of that
long performance of *Parsifal*, so as to be able to think for a while at
leisure' (*MPG*: 144). And he devotes himself to a meditation on literature,
to the discovery of the reality and truth beneath appearances: 'The
great difficulty is that a truth should be hidden thus beneath some
material thing, some simple form. How would I separate the one from
the other? And it was always thus. It was always beneath images that
I sensed precious truth . . .' (*MPG*: 168). Gradually we arrive at the
idea that *the* book should capture this moment of truth. Material

images are so many 'runes', 'hieroglyphics': 'Reading this book [would amount] to an act of creation, of resurrection, for which there is no substitute, so that for a moment (?) the very reality of life might appear. But it is also the only book that has truly dictated reality to us; and the impression it has made on us is the hallmark of its authenticity . . . This book is our only book' (*MPG*: 168–9). There follows a meditation on the works of writers whose intellect robs them of their capacity to grasp the essence of things.

It is at this point that the '*Parsifal* panel' occurs (Cahier 58, folios 29–31), a key passage from our point of view since it is a musical work and not a literary one that provides access to the truth:

Some of these truths themselves are perfectly supernatural beings whom we have never seen, but whom we recognise with infinite pleasure when a great artist succeeds in bringing them from that divine world to which he has access so that they may come to shine for a moment above our own. Was not this motif of the 'Good Friday Spell', which (doubtless through a door of the great salon left half-open because of the heat) reached me just a moment ago, providing support for my idea if indeed it had not just suggested it – was it not one of these beings, not belonging to any of the species of reality, or to any of the realms of nature, that we might conceive? With his violin bow Wagner seems to content himself with discovering this being, rendering it visible like a faded picture newly restored, revealing all its contours with the prudent and tender assurance of instruments that follow their track, now changing subtly to indicate a shadow, now marking more boldly the greater brilliance where, just for a moment before disappearing, the vision reaches – that scrupulously respected vision to which they would not have been able to add one single feature without our having felt that Wagner was embellishing, lying, ceasing to see and concealing its fading with fragments of his own invention. What exactly was its clear relationship to the first awakening of spring? Who could have said? It was still there, like an iridescent bubble that had not yet burst, like a rainbow that had faded for a moment only to begin shining again with a livelier brilliance, adding now all the tones of the prism to the mere two colours that had iridesced at the beginning and making them sing. And one remained in a silent ecstasy, as if a single gesture would have imperilled the delicious, frail presence which one wished to go on admiring for as long as it lasted and which would in a moment disappear.   (*MPG*: 172–3)[8]

Of course the work that captures these truths cannot be made up entirely of absolute essences: 'Undoubtedly such unintelligible truths, immediately perceived, are too rare for a work of art to be wholly com-

posed of them; they have to be embedded in a material that is less pure'
(*MPG*: 173). But it is indeed such truths that the writer must try to
grasp:

This truth, from the most poetic to the purely psychological, would have to
be expressed by things – language, characters, actions – that were somehow
entirely chosen and created by it, so that they might resemble it entirely, and
so that no alien word might denature it. If I had been a writer, I would have
wanted to use as material only those things in my life that had given me the
sensation of reality and not of a lie.   (*MPG*: 175)

This reality is made up of 'truly musical moments' (*ibid.*); the 'spiritual
essence' can be compared to 'the sound material of the symphony in
music, where the slightest anxiety, the most furtive shadow or the most
fleeting desire for happiness causes all the instruments to shiver, fade
or grow animated at once' (*MPG*: 177).

As early as 1910–11, then, music, and most particularly the 'Good
Friday Spell', was seen as a model for the literary enterprise: here
already we note the crucial idea – and we shall return to it – that
music is a perfect model for the workings of involuntary memory, from
which the Narrator will fashion the very stuff of his book. The passages
I have quoted already contain the themes that are developed in the
description of the Septet (that is, in *The Captive*), even as they sketch
out the famous aesthetic meditation in *Time Regained*, set in the library
of the Princesse de Guermantes. The final version will redistribute this
material into two separate episodes, but the earlier state of the text confirms the fundamental role that music plays in the quest for the artistic
absolute and in the Narrator's decision to realise the vocation of a
writer.

I believe it can be argued, therefore, that even before writing 'Swann
in Love' in 1912 Proust had the end of his book in mind: the artistic
revelation provided by a musical work, *Parsifal*. Why, then, was he to
suppress this fragment on the 'Spell' in the final version of *Time
Regained*?

First we may reconstruct the chronology of the work's genesis. In
1912 Proust completes 'Swann in love', at least in the typescript which
he submits, together with 'Combray', to Grasset and which is refused.
In it we find a character named Vington, a scientific researcher, as well
as another named Berget, composer of the Sonata (Yoshikawa 1979:

293). It is around May 1913, as the same critic shows (1979: 294), that the Vington of Combray becomes first Vindeuil, then Vinteuil, in the second proofs. Bonnet (*MPG*: 277) has managed to establish that the first rough draft for the Septet, where the work is a quartet − a draft which is to be found among the notes for *Time Regained* (written between 1913 and 1916, and published by Bonnet in *MPG*: 292–6) − can be dated precisely to the last quarter of 1914: it was intended to replace the description of the 'Good Friday Spell', as is plain from the number of identical phrases. Then there are the vacillations between quintet, sextet and septet that can be discerned in the first version of the Septet episode (Cahier 55, written *c*. 1915), as also in the notebooks of the fair copy (Yoshikawa 1979); signs of these vacillations are still evident in the first Pléiade edition. Thus it is shortly *after* having written the rough draft of *Time Regained* with which we are concerned (1910–11) that Proust completes 'Swann in love', in 1912, and introduces the character of Vinteuil. He then has the starting-point of his quest. We may conclude that the draft of the 'transmission' scene published by the *Figaro littéraire* was written between 1912 and 1914 (the date of the first version of the Septet, as a quartet).

Once Proust had had the idea that the Narrator's revelation of the artistic absolute would come to him through the medium of a work of music, and that this work would be an expansion of the Sonata which had been the cause of Swann's failure, there was no longer any reason for him to keep a specific reference to *Parsifal* in *Time Regained*. The Narrator had to experience his revelation through an *imaginary* work of art, for according to the logic of the novel a real work always disappoints: attainment of the absolute could only be suggested by a work that was unrealised, unreal and ideal. Moreover, this work had to be a piece of *pure music* whose content was not conveyed through words: because of this, a fragment from an opera (and we are not told that it is being played in its symphonic, concert version, since this is the first Paris performance of *Parsifal*'s 'second' act) would have been unsuitable. The work could not even be the Franck Quartet, which was explicitly cited in the dedication to Lacretelle, as we have seen. The redemptive work cannot be of this world.

In the event, Proust introduces the 'real' Wagner into the passage of *The Captive* that I took as my starting-point (see above, pp. 12ff.). This passage occurs at a very specific point of the quest: the point where the work of art, even a sublime one, still appears too 'artificial' and cannot aspire to purity.[9]

Thus Wagner emerges as a principal source of Proust's thinking. He provides him with a mirror image of his own poietics and − in a slightly narcissistic way − of a creative *alter ego*; moreover, he supplies him, at an earlier stage in the genesis of the novel, with a work which tells of a quest analogous to that of *A la recherche* and which could, by association, be the work that inspires the Narrator's revelation of the absolute. In his notes of 1913–16 Proust writes: 'I shall present the discovery of Time regained in the sensations induced by the spoon, the tea, etc., as an illumination à la Parsifal' (*MPG*: 318). But let us beware. This statement tells us quite clearly that *Parsifal*, or the 'Good Friday Spell', is the work that *recounts* the quest for the absolute; it cannot any longer be the work that, in itself, *touches on* the absolute. This was a further reason for eliminating it from this crucial moment of *A la recherche*.

The psychological progression embodied in *A la recherche* parallels that of *Parsifal*. It is no accident that, as we have seen, the idea of the 'blossoming girls' was already present at the time of *Contre Sainte-Beuve*. The Narrator is delayed in his quest by the girls just as Parsifal is by the Flower Maidens. Thus there is no doubt whatever, in my view, that the passages of *Within a Budding Grove* in which Proust describes girls in terms of flowers were inspired by Wagner. Swann, like Amfortas, has let himself be trapped in the snares of love. Does not Proust associate Odette − and, with her, all the other temptresses, her daughter Gilberte, Mme de Guermantes, Albertine − with Kundry, the prisoner of the magician Klingsor, when he writes, shortly before the 'transmission' scene: 'I should have been less ill at ease in a magician's cave than in this little waiting-room where the fire appeared to me to be performing alchemical transmutations as in Klingsor's laboratory' (*WBG*, I: 567–8)?[10] It is only when the Narrator succeeds in passing beyond the illusions of romantic love, particularly after the distressing experience of Albertine's kiss (*G*, II: 379), that he can gain access to the revelation, just as Parsifal, after being kissed by Kundry, is able to comprehend the mystery of the Grail and succeed where Amfortas has failed. Parsifal attains to perfect understanding at the time of the Good Friday spell; the Narrator, when listening to the Septet. Parsifal is able to enter Monsalvat, led by Gurnemanz; the Narrator, the library of the Princesse de Guermantes.[11] One cannot fail to note that, in both cases, the revelation takes place after a *walk* which is the concrete realisation of the quest. Wagner laid great stress upon the ascent to the Grail, symbolised by the visible unrolling of the scenery in the first, 1882 production; and in Proust the episode of the uneven paving-stones in the courtyard, leading to the illumination in the library, comes precisely at the end of a long walk in Paris.

The name Swann, which 'had for me become almost mythological' (*S*, I: 157), was surely not chosen by accident, so close is it to the German *Schwann*. As Rousset has emphasised (1962: 149), the Narrator, having had to choose between the Swann/Charlus pair and the Elstir/Vinteuil pair, sides decisively with the creative artists. He 'eliminates once and for all Swann and Charlus, who lived on in him and threatened to make him sterile': just as Parsifal kills the swan the hunt for which has led him to Monsalvat, where he will experience a revelation, so the Narrator stops following in the footsteps of Swann only to be confronted, in Swann's house, by the Sonata that will lead him to artistic truth.

One is also struck by the close analogy between the reaction of the Narrator, exposed for the first time to the Sonata whose religious character has been carefully evoked in the course of the Saint-Euverte soirée, and the reaction of Parsifal, who witnesses a ceremony which he does not understand. Proust was well acquainted with this scene. In a letter to Jacques Rivière (17 February 1914) about the unity of his work, he wrote: 'It would be just as if a spectator who saw Parsifal, at the end of the first act, understanding nothing of the ceremony and being chased off by Gurnemanz, were to suppose that what Wagner had meant was that simplicity of heart leads to nothing.' Like *Parsifal*, *A la recherche* is a work whose hero is on a quest for redemption. But just as Amfortas fails the first time around, it is not Swann but the Narrator who will succeed.

Yet *Parsifal* is also something else. This work is, according to Wagner's thinking, what Proust hoped *A la recherche* would be: a redemptive work. For these two works of Wagner and Proust are not content with telling the story of a quest. They seek to convey a message of salvation. The pilgrimage to Bayreuth, the sacred hill, the mystic abyss: of course there were contemporaries of Wagner who smiled, but Wagner considered himself without question to be the apostle of a new artistic religion, and even today there are admirers of Wagner whose attitude towards his work is typically mystical and religious. As far as Proust is concerned, critics have talked of 'art religion', and every year there is a pilgrimage of Proustians to Illiers at the time when the hawthorn flowers bloom. There is no doubt whatever that, for Proust, *A la recherche* preached the eminent dignity of art, which had the capacity to snatch away those who understood it from the difficulties and disappointments of life.

Proust could hardly have accorded to the work of someone else, therefore, the revelatory function he reserved for his own. Thus the work that underlay the fundamental axis of his novel – the revelation through music which leads the Narrator to his vocation as a writer – can yield its place all the more easily to a work at once absolute and imaginary, the Septet, because a new work of redemption, *A la recherche*, exists and because this new work has assimilated its message, function and content.

We must now show how, in Proust's description of the works of Vinteuil, the different themes are related one to another and so lead to the final revelation, as well as how this is rendered possible in the author's mind through the very specific nature of musical language.

3

Music as redemptive model for literature

In Proust the quest for the artistic absolute passes through three stages. At first the character does not understand the work; confronted by this enigma, he embarks upon a search for explanations, which turn out to be illusory; however, once beyond this second stage of false trails, he is able to penetrate to the essence of the work.[1]

This general progression in three stages, which characterises both Swann's attempt and the Narrator's quest, is also found in the description of Vinteuil's works themselves. At first the work appears impressionistic, a pure magma of sound in which vague elements of description can be recognised; then, as the outlines get clearer and the references more precise, the work becomes frankly descriptive, conveying ideas through individualised musical motifs and assuming a quasi-linguistic status; finally, the work passes beyond this stage in order to arrive at a pure play of sonorous forms and achieve profundity.

These three stages correspond in turn to Proust's three modes of musical perception. At first perception is blurred and indistinct; then the rational intellect intervenes, seeking to understand the work in several ways; finally, perception rises above the intellectual level to the point where it is purified and capable of apprehending a truth.

The whole process is accompanied by a progressive conception of music which may legitimately be called semiological: at each stage music maintains a certain type of symbolic relationship with the external world, and if, at the final level, it becomes possible for the Narrator to see in music the example of what a literary work should be, this is not simply because the Septet rehearses the innumerable preparations, reminiscences and connections which, according to Proust, are supposed to characterise a novel; it is also and above all because music constitutes a particular type of language which can serve as a model for literature.

*

*   *

We know very little about musical perception, even though current research in this field is particularly concentrated. How are we to understand what happens within us when we listen to music? Through our own study of a score, or by analysing other people's impressions? Every method is difficult and yields uneven results. But it is possible to envisage a careful study of how writers talk about their perception of music.

Now, Proust reveals himself to be a particularly sensitive witness. Saint-Loup says to the Narrator at Balbec: 'The hotel . . . is more or less adapted to your auditory hyperaesthesia' (G, II: 69), and the Narrator himself speaks of 'our hearing, that delightful sense' (C, III: 111). Any reader who is aware of the difficulties of analysing musical perception can only admire the acuteness of a remark such as the following, in which Proust identifies the influence of visual perception on auditory perception: 'There are in the music of the violin − if one does not see the instrument itself, and so cannot relate what one hears to its [physical] form, which modifies the tone − accents . . .' (S, I: 378).

At the beginning of the passage devoted to sessions on the pianola, significantly the last devoted to Vinteuil − as if it were a resumé of all previous musical experience − we read the following:

[Albertine] chose pieces which were either quite new or which she had played to me only once or twice, for, beginning to know me better, she was aware that I liked to fix my thoughts only upon what was still obscure to me, and to be able, in the course of these successive renderings, thanks to the increasing but, alas, distorting and alien light of my intellect, to link to one another the fragmentary and interrupted lines of the structure which at first had been almost hidden in mist. She knew and, I think, understood the joy that my mind derived, at these first hearings, from this task of modelling a still shapeless nebula . . . She guessed that at the third or fourth repetition my intellect, having grasped, having consequently placed at the same distance, all the parts, and no longer having to exert any effort on them, had conversely projected and immobilised them on a uniform plane. She did not, however, yet move on to another piece, for, without perhaps having any clear idea of the process that was going on inside me, she knew that at the moment when the exertions of my intellect* had succeeded in dispelling the mystery of a work, it was very rarely that, in compensation, it had not, in the course of its baleful task, picked up some profitable reflexion. And when in time Albertine said: 'We might give this roll to Françoise and get her to change it for something else,' often there was for me a piece of music the less in the world, perhaps, but a truth the more.

(*C*, III: 378-9)

Here the development of ideas is crucial, for Proust is describing the three stages in which perceptual penetration of a work takes place:

(1) At first the Narrator likes to hear something new, something unknown to him. He is immediately confronted by a *nebula*, yet one which represents a challenge.
(2) A challenge to the intellect, for it is the intellect that seizes hold of the work in order to penetrate its mystery. This is an essential stage, but it is also a relatively negative one. The intellect is 'distorting and alien'; it calls on the resources of reason; it weaves fragmentary elements together and 'flattens them out', or, in other words, transforms the work into an object. It is this that allows the listener to give free rein to his subjectivity.
(3) Yet once this stage has been passed – although the mystery has gone and the work may even disappear – the intellect has cleared the way to a transcendent truth.

Musical perception in Proust, the foundation of the progressive penetration of a work, is therefore something that is inscribed in time. Understanding is a process, a kind of 'task'; and this task is carried out in three dimensions of time, which correspond, of course, to the three stages I have identified:

(a) at the level of the work heard for the first time – one understands the end of a work better than its beginning;
(b) at the level of repeated hearings of the same work – a difficult

---

* *Intelligence.* This work is translated variously by Scott Moncrieff and Kilmartin as 'intelligence', 'intellect' and 'the human mind'. Here they opt for 'intelligence', even though they have translated *intelligence* as 'intellect' twice earlier in the same paragraph. Since *intelligence* is a central concept in the discussion that follows, I have translated it consistently as 'intellect', changing the Scott Moncrieff/Kilmartin text where necessary to bring it into line. (Such changes are always footnoted.) For a discussion of Schopenhauer's distinction between intellect and intuition, see below, p. 80. [Trans.]

work cannot be understood immediately, one has to come back to it, go a little more deeply into it each time one hears it;

(c) at the level of the long term − great works create their own posterity, which can require decades, even centuries, of listening.

At first hearing, the work remains opaque. Swann, at the time of the 'archetypal' performance, is unable to distinguish between the little phrase and its harmony, and does not manage to perceive an outline (*S*, I: 227). This initial situation will later be recalled at the Saint-Euverte soirée: 'There were in this passage some admirable ideas which Swann had not distinguished on first hearing' (*S*, I: 382). The same phenomenon is experienced by the Narrator: 'But often one hears nothing when one listens for the first time to a piece of music that is at all complicated' (*WBG*, I: 570); or again, 'even when I had heard the sonata from beginning to end, it remained almost wholly invisible to me' (*ibid.*: 571).

But the work unfolds in time. Even when one first hears it, memory intervenes to establish connections between its various parts, so that understanding of the work evolves during the course of its performance. This is Swann's experience even at the very beginning of his initial encounter with the Sonata:

the notes themselves have vanished before these sensations have developed sufficiently to escape submersion under those which the succeeding or even simultaneous notes have already begun to awaken in us. And this impression would continue to envelop in its liquidity, its ceaseless overlapping, the motifs which from time to time emerge, barely discernible, to plunge again and disappear and drown, recognised only by the particular kind of pleasure which they instil, impossible to describe, to recollect, to name, ineffable − did not our memory, like a labourer who toils at the laying down of firm foundations beneath the tumult of the waves, by fashioning for us facsimiles of those fugitive phrases, enable us to compare and to contrast them with those that follow. And so, scarcely had the exquisite sensation which Swann had experienced died away, before his memory had furnished him with an immediate transcript, sketchy, it is true, and provisional, which he had been able to glance at while the piece continued, so that, when the same impression suddenly returned, it was no longer impossible to grasp.   (*S*, I: 228)

This 'intervention of memory', itself indissolubly bound up with time, is also found to operate between separate hearings of the same work. Those ideas which Swann had not distinguished on first hearing 'he now perceived, as if, in the cloak-room of his memory, they had divested themselves of the uniform disguise of their novelty' (*S*, I: 382). As for the Narrator:

And yet when, later on, this sonata had been played to me two or three times I found that I knew it perfectly well . . . Probably what is wanting, the first time, is not comprehension but memory. For our memory, relatively to the complexity of the impressions which it has to face while we are listening, is infinitesimal . . . Of these multiple impressions our memory is not capable of furnishing us with an immediate picture. But that picture gradually takes shape in the memory.   (*WBG*, I: 570)

Time, then, far from being that enemy who gnaws away at people and, in so doing, alters the image we have of them, proves to be essential for our understanding and appreciation of works of art. Posterity demands a sustained effort: 'The time, moreover, that a person requires – as I required in the case of this sonata – to penetrate a work of any depth is merely an epitome, a symbol, one might say, of the years, the centuries even, that must elapse before the public can begin to cherish a masterpiece that is really new' (*WBG*, I: 572).

Here – and this is highly relevant – Proust cites Beethoven as an example:

It was Beethoven's quartets themselves (the Twelfth, Thirteenth, Fourteenth and Fifteenth) that devoted half a century to forming, fashioning and enlarging the audience for Beethoven's quartets, thus marking, like every great work of art, an advance if not in the quality of artists at least in the community of minds, largely composed to-day of what was not to be found when the work first appeared, that is to say of persons capable of appreciating it. What is called posterity is the posterity of the work of art.   (*Ibid.*: 572)

In my view the reference to Beethoven's late quartets is no accident. I shall later try to show how and why the last movement of the Vinteuil Septet conceals a veiled allusion to Beethoven's Sixteenth Quartet, one which is of particular significance for *A la recherche*.

The above analysis provides a preliminary explanation for the fact that it is not monuments or paintings – although so important elsewhere in *A la recherche*, and especially at the beginning – but music that serves as a guiding thread for the Narrator on his journey towards aesthetic revelation: music, like the quest – and like *A la recherche* itself

– unfolds in time. Through the play of transformations, reminiscences and perceptual responses that it arouses in us, it is like a microcosm of our relation to the world as inscribed in time and as conditioned by it. In particular, music imitates, in its thematic development, the workings of involuntary memory, and this analogy is encapsulated in 'the little phrase' that returns from one movement to another in the manner of Franck's cyclic sonatas. (I shall come back to the significance of this important detail: see below, p. 63.)

Thus the descriptions of the Sonata and the Septet do not simply provide an opportunity for Proust to show how understanding moves through the successive stages of the perceptual process; they also reveal the *properties* of musical perception in his work. Perception can be seen to have three essential characteristics: it is selective, discontinuous and changeable.[2]

Selective: on reading the musical passages of *A la recherche*, one realises immediately that Proust is not at all concerned with giving a complete account of the work: rather, he describes what has struck Swann or the Narrator. The selection thus focuses on particular movements, and on specific moments within each movement.

When the Sonata is played on the piano at the Verdurins', it is in the Andante that Swann discovers the little phrase. Incidental remarks scattered throughout *A la recherche* confirm the particular predilection for this movement: ' "The Duchess must be allianced with all that lot," said Françoise, taking up the conversation again at the Guermantes of the Rue de la Chaise, as one resumes a piece of music at the andante' (*G*, II: 17). Again, M. de Charlus in *The Captive*: 'Wasn't it really beautiful? The andante, what? It's the most touching thing that was ever written' (*C*, III: 281). And further: '. . . we might request Charlie . . . to play for us alone the sublime *adagio*' (*ibid*.: 289).

Within the movement under consideration, one special moment holds the attention of Swann and the Narrator: none other than the little phrase, which in the course of the 'archetypal' performance emerges from a sort of undifferentiated magma of sound. Let us go back through the description of that performance:

(a) 'At first he had appreciated only the material quality of the sounds which those instruments secreted' (*S*, I: 227).
(b) 'But then at a certain moment, *without being able to distinguish any*

*clear outline*³ . . . he had tried to grasp the phrase or harmony – he did not know which – that had just been played' (*ibid.*: 227).

(c) '*This time he had distinguished quite clearly a phrase* which emerged for a few moments above the waves of sound' (*ibid.*: 228).

(d) 'Then it vanished. He hoped, with a passionate longing, that he might find it again, a third time. And reappear it did' (*ibid.*: 229).

In subsequent hearings, therefore, it is the little phrase that he is going to wait for and rediscover.

Thus it is not surprising that musical perception in Proust should be *discontinuous* (Piroué 1960: 139). In the first place, because when one listens to music one does not remember everything one has heard: 'The music of Vinteuil extended, note by note, stroke by stroke, the unknown, incalculable colourings of an unsuspected world, fragmented by the gaps between the different occasions of hearing his work performed' (*C*, III: 257). Secondly, because one's attention may wander on account of a weakness in the work: 'Truth to tell, this joyous motif did not appeal to me aesthetically . . . It seemed to me that Vinteuil had been lacking, here, in inspiration, and consequently I was a little lacking also in the power of attention' (*ibid.*: 252). Finally, because it is impossible to apprehend a work in its entirety – hence the need for repeated hearings: 'Since I was able to enjoy everything that this sonata had to give me only in a succession of hearings, I never possessed it in its entirety: it was like life itself. But, less disappointing than life, great works of art do not begin by giving us the best of themselves' (*WBG*, I: 571).

For musical perception is *changeable*. The Narrator does not, at first, care for the joyous motif in the Septet, but he will hear it again and learn to love it:

even within those works [works that are truly rare] . . . it is the least precious parts that one at first perceives . . . But when those first impressions have receded, there remains for our enjoyment some passage whose structure, too new and strange to offer anything but confusion to our mind, had made it indistinguishable and so preserved intact . . . we shall love it longer than the rest because we have taken longer to get to love it.   (*Ibid.*: 571–2)

It is not surprising, therefore, that the Sonata should become the object of many different descriptions which, naturally, reflect the progressive enrichment of Swann's perception – and also the various phases of his love for Odette. For the same reasons, the Narrator, when he hears the Sonata and the Septet, makes the journey that takes him from the vague and indistinct perception of first hearing, by way of the intermediate diversion of rational explanation, to the final apprehension of the aesthetic essence.

This progression in three stages will also be found in the motion that carries us along chronologically from the first hearing of the Sonata to the Septet. What matters now is to show, through a study of Proust's descriptions of these works, how each particular description can be explained by its place in the overall progression, in terms both of its sensory qualities and of the nature of the music.

*

*   *

1   The 'archetypal' performance and the Andante at the Verdurins'
(S, I: 224–34)

The description of Swann's very first experience of the Sonata is inserted into the account of the Verdurin soirée at which the pianist is asked to play 'the sonata in F sharp' in a piano arrangement.

Mme Verdurin is at her most affected: 'I don't want to be made to cry until I get a cold in the head, and neuralgia all down my face, like last time.' Proust is here indulging in a preliminary brief description of the musical snobbery prevalent among the Verdurin clan, since Mme Verdurin's reactions are understood as a sign of her musical sensitivity. It is agreed that only the Andante should be performed. Mme Verdurin then shows off her musical knowledge: 'The Master is really too priceless! Just as though, in the Ninth, he said, "we'll just hear the *finale*," or "just the overture" of the *Mastersingers*.'

Flashback: as he listens to the Andante, Swann recognises the theme of a violin sonata which he had heard the previous year and which had left a deep impression on him. Proust devotes a long passage to the confused perception Swann had had of it. Here the author combines two types of observation.

On the one hand, the qualities peculiar to the sonorous material which lead him to speak of '*purely* musical impressions': the violin line is 'slender', 'robust', 'compact' and 'commanding'; the mass of the piano part 'multiform', 'indivisible', 'smooth' yet 'restless'; the music evokes arabesques and surfaces of varied dimensions. At the beginning the sensations are of the order of 'breadth', 'tenuity', 'stability' or 'capriciousness'. Then, when perception becomes more precise, Proust introduces more objective judgments, such as 'symmetrical arrangement' and 'notation'. As for the little phrase, we are told that it is 'secret, murmuring, detached, . . . airy and perfumed . . . dancing, pastoral, interpolated, episodic'. We thus have an abundance of concrete observations, corresponding to the first impressions of a Swann literally submerged.

For − and this is the second aspect of the evocation − mixed up with these purely musical impressions, in a 'deep blue' and 'iridescent' atmosphere, we find observations which are indeed descriptive but at the same time rather vague, relating to the world of the sea: 'the mass of the piano-part beginning to emerge in a sort of liquid rippling of sound' evokes 'the deep blue tumult of the sea, silvered and charmed into a minor key by the moonlight'. The words 'submersion', 'liquidity', 'emerge', 'plunge', 'tumult of the waves' should also be noted; and the phrase is located 'above the waves of sound'.

Why this atmosphere of the sea? By way of preparation, no doubt, for the first movement of the Septet, in *The Captive*, but also because the sea is indissolubly bound up in Proust's mental geography with the emergence of woman: one has only to think of the girls on the sea-front at Balbec. The little phrase will soon be associated with an unknown woman, then more specifically with Odette.

It is not without interest, for the remainder of this discussion, to note that Proust describes this first hearing of the Sonata exactly as he would a work of Debussy. This is not only because of the fragmentary, subtle and quivering character of the sonorous material, but also because the world of the Sonata is of a delicate nature, permeated by 'the fragrance of . . . roses, wafted upon the moist air of evening', a world where the motifs are filled with 'fluidity' and everything is 'melted'. Later, in the 'transmission' scene, there will be a reference to 'haze'. And in the light of Proust's technique (to which I shall return) of supplying clues far removed from the passage where they are to be interpreted, it is noteworthy that when Odette plays the Sonata to the Narrator Proust alludes to 'impressionism', the 'pursuit of dissonance' and the *exclusive* use of the Chinese scale' − which is no doubt an exaggeration but is nonetheless characteristic of Debussy (*WBG*, I: 573).

In the passage as a whole there are two clearly distinct phases in the perception of sonorous phenomena. 'At first he had appreciated only the material quality of the sounds which those instruments secreted.' This is the realm of the inexpressible: Swann is unable 'to give a name to what was pleasing him'; the motifs are 'impossible to describe, to recollect, to name, ineffable'. A moment of pure music.

Then, when the phrase returns, he distinguishes it clearly and is able to describe it more precisely: its rhythm is slow; it changes direction after a pause; it resumes in a quicker tempo. It vanishes. It comes back a third time. At this point the intellect intervenes, suggesting *substitutes* for the sonorous form to his mind: 'He had before him *something that was no longer pure music*, but rather design, architecture, thought, and which allowed the actual music to be recalled.' Here we are on the track of what will be the essential feature of Swann's attempt to appropriate the Sonata, an attempt which will end in failure. Indeed Swann is already starting down a false trail, albeit embryonically: he falls in love with the little phrase. Personified now for the first time, it is compared to an unknown woman who is briefly met, immediately loved but never really known.

Yet the Sonata seems to offer him a second trail – the right one, from Proust's point of view, as we know if we have read the whole novel, and one that would enable Swann to transcend the life of pleasure to which he has abandoned himself: 'He had . . . long ceased to direct his life towards any ideal goal, confining himself to the pursuit of emphemeral satisfactions'. The new direction is evoked in a vague manner:

like a confirmed invalid . . . [who] begins to envisage the possibility, hitherto beyond all hope, of starting to lead belatedly a wholly different life, Swann found in himself, in the memory of the phrase that he had heard . . . the presence of one of those invisible realities in which he had ceased to believe and to which . . . he was conscious once again of the desire and almost the strength to consecrate his life.

It is one of Proust's great skills that each time he describes the Sonata he can suggest, and in a manner that is stronger with each description, this transcendent dimension towards which Swann could direct his energies but which he will never understand. That is reserved for the Narrator. Swann, instead, embarks upon another false trail, by seeking a rational explanation of the work in its relationship with the composer:

'Never having managed to find out whose work it was that he had heard played that evening, he had been unable to procure a copy and had finally forgotten the quest' – though not without having made a few enquiries about it.

The performance of the Andante at the Verdurins' enables him to identify the work. Here Proust moves beyond the stage of the inexpressible which he had been concerned to emphasise in the first description: 'But now, at last, he could ask the name of his fair unknown (and was told that it was the *andante* of Vinteuil's sonata for piano and violin); he held it safe, could have it again to himself, at home, as often as he wished, could study its language and acquire its secret.' To the extent that the passages with which we are concerned, taken together, constitute a microcosm of *A la recherche*, as most writers dealing with music in Proust have seen, it is important to stress the parallel between Swann's apprehension of the Sonata through the identification of its name and the evolution of the Narrator's quest (the latter being considered now in relation to the novel as a whole). This quest will begin, at the end of 'Swann in love', with a reflection on the names of Balbec, and then the knowledge of Balbec itself – just as, later, the Narrator's meditation on the name Guermantes will precede his actual meeting with the Duchess. Indeed, everything, including even the theme of 'the captive', who is first captured by her name, is already present here.

Swann continues with his enquiries: 'He asked for information about this Vinteuil: what else he had done, at what period in his life he had composed the sonata, and what meaning the little phrase could have had for him – that was what Swann wanted most to know.' What is Swann doing? He is asking exactly the same sort of questions about music as Sainte-Beuve asked about literature; he is making the mistake of trying to understand the work through the biography of its author, the circumstances of its creation and the intentions of the composer. We are thus right at the very heart of the problematic of *A la recherche*, since the novel grew out of *Contre-Sainte-Beuve*, as we have seen, and will include, in the theoretical and aesthetic section of *Time Regained*, a condemnation of this type of critical approach: there Proust will denounce

the futility of those critical essays which try to guess who it is that an author is talking about. A work, even one that is directly autobiographical, is at the very least put together out of several intercalated episodes in the life of the author – earlier episodes which have inspired the work and later ones which resemble it just as much, the later loves being traced after the pattern of the earlier.   (*TR*, III: 945–6)

Later he will also poke fun at 'historians of music' [*musicographes*] who search for the origins of styles (*C*, III: 257).

All this in the middle of the mundane and superficial chatter of Mme Verdurin: 'Though it's better, really, than an orchestra, more complete . . . But you don't dare to confess that you don't know Vinteuil's sonata; you have no right not to know it! . . . No, we don't waste time splitting hairs in this house.' In fact the members of the clan understand nothing of the work: 'It appeared to them, when the pianist played his sonata, as though he were striking at random from the piano a medley of notes which bore no relation to the musical forms to which they themselves were accustomed.' And so Swann learns that the Vinteuil Sonata had 'caused a great stir among the most advanced school of musicians': this informs us that we are dealing with a work of some significance, for Proust's tone here is not ironic. The passage ends with a description of Vinteuil's illness. The painter 'Master' Biche (Elstir), who is present among the guests, claims that it is possible to detect in the work signs of the composer's mental derangement. This brings us back to the question of the relationship between the creative artist and his work, yet Swann remains merely perplexed:

This remark did not strike Swann as ridiculous; but it disturbed him, for, since *a work of pure music* contains none of the logical sequences whose deformation, in spoken or written language, is a proof of insanity, so insanity diagnosed in a sonata seemed as mysterious a thing as the insanity of a dog or a horse, although instances may be observed of these.

It is important to emphasise the way in which Swann's questions are mixed up with descriptions of the reactions of the members of the Verdurin clan. For Proust is here outlining a typology of the musical (and artistic) public, and one which also exists on three levels: the snobs who do not understand but behave as if they do; the cultivated amateur who makes an effort to penetrate the work but remains, like the critic and the musicologist, at the mere stage of rational enquiry; and the man of the élite who will enter upon the scene only later and achieve authentic understanding. Even this hierarchy of the public, then, corresponds to the three stages of Proustian perception and the three phases of the aesthetic quest.

The actual performance at the Verdurins' as such is described much more briefly than the 'archetypal' performance. Proust pretends to give us the means to identify the little phrase: 'After a high note sustained through two whole bars, Swann sensed its approach, stealing forth from beneath that long-drawn sonority, stretched like a curtain of sound to veil the mystery of its incubation, and recognised, secret, murmuring, detached, the airy and perfumed phrase that he had loved.' Its characteristics have not really changed. Proust wants above all to recall the theme of the analogy between the little phrase and an unknown woman whom one desires to meet again; and this parallel, stated a second time, prepares us for the identification of the phrase with Odette which constitutes the central point of the next passages.

2 *Other Verdurin performances (S, I: 238–9)*

The playing on the piano of the little phrase alone, the 'national anthem' of the love of Swann and Odette, becomes a sort of ritual. Proust is especially concerned to link his description of this with the growth of their feelings: the little phrase will gradually become more familiar to us. However, a new theme appears, one which needs to be related both to the general growth in musical understanding on the characters' part and to the respective role of the arts in the evolution of the novel: the comparison of the Sonata with painting:

[The pianist] would begin with the sustained tremolos of the violin part which for several bars were heard alone, filling the whole foreground; until suddenly they seemed to draw aside, and – *as in those interiors by Pieter de Hooch which are deepened by the narrow frame of a half-opened door*, in the far distance, of a different colour, velvety with the radiance of some intervening light – the little phrase appeared, dancing, pastoral, interpolated, episodic, belonging to another world.

Through this explicit comparison with the pictorial representation of a Dutch interior, the Sonata clearly acquires, if only indirectly, a descriptively precise character which it lacked in the vagueness of the previous passage. Proust thus gives it an intermediate semiological status which he will recall at the beginning of his description of the Septet – only in order, there, to surpass it.

Each of the words he uses constitutes a preparation for the later episode. He mentions a second colour which is not specified; the epithets 'dancing', 'interpolated' and 'episodic' prolong the adjectives 'secret', 'murmuring' and 'detached' from the preceding description; and they also define the *autonomy* of the little phrase, which becomes increasingly remarkable both in its appearance and in the way it is inserted into the movement, so that it will soon manage to function like a leitmotif. The word 'perfumed' in the previous description had brought the Sonata close, albeit very discreetly, to the world of plants. In the 'archetypal' performance it had been compared to the 'fragrance of certain roses'. Here it is described as 'pastoral'. This theme will be taken up again and amplified in connection with the Septet. Proust also makes a new point in suggesting that it 'belong[s] to another world'. This, together with the word 'immortal', which follows, lends the Sonata a religious dimension which is of fundamental importance and will be developed in the course of the Saint-Euverte soirée.

For the moment, what matters most is again the feminine personification of the little phrase: 'It rippled past, simple and immortal, scattering on every side the bounties of its grace, with the same ineffable smile'. But already Swann feels ambivalent towards it: he 'thought that he could now discern in it some disenchantment. It seemed to be aware how vain, how hollow was the happiness to which it showed the way' – while at the same time it is 'a pledge, a token of his love'. Here Swann experiences something important: because of the autonomy it has acquired, the little phrase has taken on the meaning of the amorous context in which he has appropriated it.

Having identified its name, he no longer seeks its meaning by way of Vinteuil but defines it in relation to his own feelings. This is the second false trail, for he is only projecting onto the phrase his emotional states, which are always changing – hence the variability of the ideas it evokes for him.

However, as before, Proust takes care to hint at the path that Swann should follow. While being a token of frailty for the future, the little phrase also possesses a dimension of its own, as if it were untouched by the contingent situation which causes him to value it: 'He almost regretted that it had a meaning of its own, an intrinsic and unalterable beauty, extraneous to themselves'. Once again Swann has the intuition of a transcendent content but does not get beyond it.

3   *The Sonata played on the piano by Odette (S, I: 258–60)*

This passage, in which Odette plays the little phrase on the piano at Swann's request – and not very well – reaffirms the two themes of the preceding passage: 'The little phrase continued to be associated in Swann's mind with his love for Odette'; and 'in so far as Odette's affection might seem a little abrupt and disappointing, the little phrase would come to supplement it, to blend with it *its own mysterious essence*'. There is something basically pathetic about the character of Swann: the little phrase, with its fundamentally sorrowful expression, could warn him of the illusory character of his love, that is, confirm that 'Odette's qualities were not such as to justify his setting so high a value on the hours he spent in her company'. But he makes nothing of it: 'What matter though the phrase repeated that love is frail and fleeting, when his love was so strong!' And the passage ends with a shower of exchanged kisses.

This lack of insight is all the more regrettable in that Swann's relationship with music is far from superficial. He knows he is confronted by a mystery which he must penetrate: 'The pleasure which the music gave him, which was shortly to create in him a real need, was in fact akin at such moments to the pleasure which he would have derived from experimenting with perfumes, from entering into contact with a world for which we men were not made'. Music belongs to a transcendent universe which remains inaccessible. Once again Swann is on the right track, for he is looking for the sense of the music beyond its rational content: 'And since he sought in the little phrase for a meaning to which his intellect* could not descend, with what a strange frenzy of intoxication did he *strip bare his innermost soul of the whole armour of reason* and make it pass unattended through the dark filter of sound!' But he gains nothing from all this: Swann gets bogged down on the false trail of his love for Odette. This passage is an important link in Proust's 'demonstration', since it will be necessary for the Narrator, too, to experience the disappointments of love – an experience which

---

* 'Intelligence' in Scott Moncrieff/Kilmartin. [Trans.]

he, however, will overcome, in order to discover in the music of Vinteuil the path to the true life.

4   The Sonata played on the piano at the Verdurins' (S, I: 288); the little phrase on the outskirts of Paris (ibid.: 295)

As the amorous relationship between Swann and Odette evolves, the little phrase is coloured with new situations. M. de Forcheville – who will be the lover and then the second husband of Odette – has been introduced by her into the Verdurin salon. 'Swann, in his heart of hearts, turned to it [the little phrase] as to a confidant of his love, as to a friend of Odette who would surely tell her to pay no attention to this Forcheville.' The little phrase 'betrays' him because it tells him only what he wants to hear: Swann continues to make the mistake of associating with it his love for Odette, even though he should already have good reason to distrust it.

This provides an opportunity for Proust to round out his description of the phrase, without, however, altering its general appearance:

Beneath the restless tremolos of the violin part which protected it with their throbbing *sostenuto* two octaves above it – and as in a mountainous country, behind the seeming immobility of a vertiginous waterfall, one descries, two hundred feet below, the tiny form of a woman walking in the valley – the little phrase had just appeared, distant, graceful, protected by the long, gradual unfurling of its transparent, incessant and sonorous curtain.

Here Proust fuses the curtain image introduced at the time of the first Verdurin performance (S, I: 230) with the sea atmosphere which has been present ever since the 'archetypal' performance, but which now has an absolute pictorial precision – we discern 'a woman walking in the valley' – acquired from when the phrase was played to Swann and Odette on the piano (*ibid.*: 238).

A brief allusion is made to the performance of the phrase on the piano when Swann dines on the outskirts of Paris. Here the same snobbish attitude prevails: the piano is brought down for him, even though he is already in disgrace with the Verdurins. There is an important point here which Proust will later develop: these performances take place, whether Swann is aware of the fact or not, amid a mass of leaves – once again the context of plants – and by moonlight, an image already introduced at the very beginning (S, I: 227).

And two pages before he is finally excluded from the Verdurin salon, Swann associates music with the role of 'procuress' which it seems to play between Odette and M. de Forcheville (*S*, I: 313). It follows that the work incriminated at this point is not the Vinteuil Sonata – indissolubly bound up with Swann and Odette – but a real work, in this case Beethoven's 'Moonlight' Sonata (*S*, I: 310, 313). The moonlight theme has, as we know, already been heard twice.

5   *The Sonata played on piano and violin at the Saint-Euverte soirée (S, I: 375–84)*

Odette has left Swann. Swann, already convinced of the futility of the Verdurin salon, is no more at ease at the Marquise de Saint-Euverte's: 'He suffered greatly from being shut up among all these people whose stupidity and absurdities struck him all the more painfully since, being ignorant of his love . . . they made it appear to him in the aspect of a subjective state which existed for himself alone, whose reality there was nothing external to confirm'. Yet here at this soirée is the Sonata being played in its entirety, on piano and violin, just as on the occasion of the 'archetypal' performance. The wheel has turned full circle, and the Saint-Euverte performance prompts a description of the last stage of understanding – a cul de sac – into which the Sonata leads him.

While Swann is lamenting the absence of Odette, the little phrase played on the violin triggers off an example of involuntary memory analogous to that of the madeleine. It reminds him not only of Odette and his love for her, but also of the wretched state to which she has brought him and which he recognises. The description sums up the emotional phases associated with the little phrase, adding the one that Swann has now reached: 'Had it not often been the witness of their joys? True that, as often, it had warned him of their frailty. And indeed, whereas in that earlier time he had divined an element of suffering in its smile, in its limpid, disenchanted tones, *tonight* he found there rather the grace of a resignation that was almost gay.' From Proust's perspective, Swann has thus reached a positive stage: not only has he recognised the disillusions of love, but he has accepted them as inevitable. The passage concludes with his acknowledging 'that the feeling which Odette had once had for him would never revive, that his hopes of happiness would not be realised now'.

The memory of his feelings for Odette, then, crowds out everything else. It is for this reason that the sonorous qualities of the little phrase, though certainly present, are much less in evidence than before: 'light, soothing, murmurous', 'a clouded surface', 'a frigid and withdrawn sweetness'. What is more important is to evoke its delicacy and frailty.

The main issue now is that music has acquired a quasi-linguistic status, with the little phrase '*telling* him what she had to *say* [to him], every *word* of which he closely scanned, regretful to see them fly away so fast'. 'Swann had regarded musical motifs as actual ideas', even if the codification involved could not 'be resolved into rational discourse'. It is no accident, then, that it should be at this point in the texts relating to Vinteuil that we find the first explicit comparison with Wagner: 'Vinteuil's phrase, like some theme, say, in *Tristan*, which represents to us also a certain emotional accretion . . . had endued a vesture of humanity that was peculiarly affecting.' This is as far as Swann gets on his journey; and it is here that the Narrator will set off, in the passage from *The Captive* discussed at the beginning of chapter 2.

Proust seems here to have captured miraculously all the ambiguity, but at the same time all the reality, of musical symbolism. The 'ideas' conveyed by the motifs are 'veiled in shadow' and 'impenetrable to the intellect',* but they are 'none the less perfectly distinct from one another, unequal among themselves in value and significance'. This to the extent that Swann is capable of identifying in the musical material itself that which corresponds to the feelings he associates with it: 'He had observed that it was to the closeness of the intervals between the five notes which composed it and to the constant repetition of two of them that was due that impression of a frigid and withdrawn sweetness . . .' In the remaining part of the sentence, Proust achieves a power of comprehension concerning the symbolic workings of music which one might wish were more widespread among musicologists: ' . . . in reality he knew that he was basing this conclusion [*raisonnait*, literally '*reasoning*'] *not upon the phrase itself*, but merely upon certain equivalents, *substituted (for the convenience of his intellect)*† for the mysterious entity of which he had become aware'. What Proust is

---

* 'Human mind' in Scott Moncrieff/Kilmartin. [Trans.]
† 'For his mind's convenience' in Scott Moncrieff/Kilmartin. [Trans.]

suggesting here is that the musical 'fact' under consideration is not a given piece of data but a construction elaborated by the rational intellect in the course of the perceptual process. From Proust's perspective of the quest, however, this type of perception is still too analytical, in that it is capable of discerning the detail of the notes which provoke the sensation: Swann is a critic, not an artist. The intellect has to pass beyond the stage of reason in order to perceive the essence.

For the moment, the Sonata appears as an equivalent of language:

How beautiful the dialogue which Swann now heard between piano and violin, at the beginning of the last passage! The suppression of human speech, so far from letting fancy reign there uncontrolled (as one might have thought), had eliminated it altogether; never was spoken language so inexorably determined, never had it known questions so pertinent, such irrefutable replies.

An equivalent of human language, but one which functions in a superior way to it and surpasses it. The reference to *St Francis of Assisi Preaching to the Birds* a little earlier (*S*, I: 357) now assumes its full significance. In the legend set to music by Liszt, the language of birds transcends human language, and it is for this reason that a saint, no less, is their interlocutor. At the Saint-Euverte soirée, the language of music is compared to a dialogue of birds, embodied by piano and violin; but it is also a language freed from words, whose significance Swann senses without really understanding it.

This association of music and language is established at a critical point in the evolution of music in *A la recherche*, as in the structure of *A la recherche* itself. Music actually acquires this linguistic status, which already embraces more than just verbal language, *after* it has been identified with painting (cf. *S*, I: 238). I believe there is a parallel here with the semiological status of music in relation to pictorial art. While references to painting abound in *Swann's Way*, where they are most especially associated with the first appearance of characters or with their first appearance to the Narrator, the frequency of such references decreases from *Cities of the Plain* onwards. It is the Septet, in *The Captive* (though the first movement of the work is merely descriptive), that becomes the instrument of revelation, owing to the particular, transcendent nature of musical language.

Only by taking note of the order in which the arts succeed each other in *A la recherche* can one understand their status. Thus I think it necessary to qualify the view of Butor, who believes he can discern in the work a 'music – painting – language' progression which corresponds, according to him, 'to the progression made up of the Sonata, the works of Elstir and *A la recherche du temps perdu*. At this point painting appears as a *middle term* between music and words' (1971: 143). Matters are in fact more complex: the identification of music with painting corresponds to an intermediate stage, of frankly descriptive music, which stands between the pure, vague music of the outset and the linguistic status of music just described, and which will be surpassed, once and for all, later, when music has attained its full, transcendent dimension. In this sense painting *precedes* music in Proust's hierarchy of the arts. Similarly the works of Elstir, notably *Carquethuit Harbour*, appear after the Narrator's first, unproductive encounter with the Sonata but well before his encounter with the Septet. Hence it is music that will be the model for literature, and the order in which the arts succeed each other ought to be: painting – music – literature.

It is no accident that in the pages leading up to the Saint-Euverte performance Proust, reaffirming the close connection between microcosm and macrocosm in his work, should cite the following real works of art in this order: *The Vices and Virtues* of Giotto (*S*, I: 357), an aria from Gluck's *Orfeo* played on the flute, Liszt's piano piece *St Francis of Assisi Preaching to the Birds* (*ibid.*: 357) – Matoré and Mecz have shown that these last two pieces symbolise music and language respectively (1972: 92), though the language is a sublimated one, since it is translated into music – and, further on, a Chopin prelude (*S*, I: 361), which, coming where it does in relation to the previous pieces, foreshadows the final transition (in the Septet) to music as a play of forms:

[Mme de Cambremer][4] had learned in her girlhood to fondle and cherish those long sinuous phrases of Chopin, so free, so flexible, so tactile, which begin by reaching out and exploring far outside and away from the direction in which they started, far beyond the point which one might have expected their notes to reach, and which divert themselves in those byways of fantasy only to return more deliberately – with a more premeditated reprise, with more precision, as on a crystal bowl that reverberates to the point of making you cry out – to strike at your heart.

Swann, however, will not reach this stage of 'essential' music, even if music offers 'an immeasurable keyboard (still almost entirely unknown)' beyond the five notes to which he assigns a meaning, beyond the seven basic notes of the scale. It is still Vinteuil he would like to find behind the Sonata: 'What could his life have been? From the depths of what well of sorrow could he have drawn that god-like strength, that unlimited power of creation?' And yet he has never gone so far in his penetration of the little phrase. For although Swann has sensed a transcendent dimension ever since the time of the first descriptions, he now puts his finger on it: 'Swann had regarded musical motifs as actual ideas, *of another world, of another order,* ideas veiled in shadow, unknown, *impenetrable to the intellect,* * but none the less perfectly distinct from one another, unequal among themselves in value and significance.' The musical motifs do indeed convey meanings in the manner of a leitmotif, but something surpasses them: the ideas Proust is speaking of here are Platonic ones. Hence later: 'It [the little phrase] yet belonged to an order of *supernatural beings* whom we have never seen, but whom, in spite of that, we recognise and acclaim with rapture when some *explorer of the unseen* contrives to coax one forth, to bring it down, from that *divine* world to which he has access, to shine for a brief moment in the firmament of ours.' The mystical atmosphere in which this passage is bathed cannot be too heavily stressed: the instrumentalists, like officiants, are performing a *rite*; they utter the *incantations* necessary to *evoke* music; music is a protective *goddess*, even if her smile contains an element of suffering; the body of the violinist is as if *possessed*; his appearance derives from a *supernatural presence*; and the platform becomes an *altar* for a *supernatural ceremony*. In addition, thanks to Proust's use of colour, the Sonata is not far from transforming itself into a septet:

It was still there, like an iridescent bubble that floats for a while unbroken. As a *rainbow* whose brightness is fading seems to subside, then soars again and, before it is extinguished, shines forth with greater splendour than it has ever shown; so to the *two colours* which the little phrase had hitherto allowed to appear it added others now, chords shot with every hue in the *prism*, and made them sing.

We are on the way to the mixture of the seven colours which, in the description of the Septet, will suggest a White Sonata. Whiteness, the rainbow: all this reinforces the image of the Sonata as a *complete* work,

---

* 'Human mind' in Scott Moncrieff/Kilmartin. [Trans.]

and one therefore that is capable of providing Swann with the revelation. I pointed out above that we were in the presence of a cyclic sonata: as in Franck, the same theme – the 'little phrase' – returns from movement to movement. Even if the revelation comes about through the Septet, the sum of all Vinteuil's previous works, the totality of totalities, nevertheless the Sonata possesses all the qualities necessary to play the role of mystical intermediary. Swann, then, has truth within his grasp but does not know it. He returns to his study of Vermeer, and we understand that he will not be able to finish it. Swann has let slip the fundamental message that the Sonata could give him, even though he has had a presentiment of it. He will not be an artist. He will not even be a critic.

The transition from Swann to the Narrator is discussed explicitly by Proust, but much later, when he makes his very last reference to the Sonata in *Time Regained*:

Thinking again of the extra-temporal joy which I had been made to feel by the sound of the spoon or the taste of the madeleine, I said to myself: 'Was this perhaps that happiness which the little phrase of the sonata promised to Swann and which he, because he was unable to find it in artistic creation, mistakenly assimilated to the pleasures of love, was this the happiness of which long ago I was given a presentiment – as something more supraterrestrial even than the mood evoked by the little phrase of the sonata – by the call, the mysterious, rubescent call of that septet which Swann was never privileged to hear, having died like so many others before the truth that was made for him had been revealed? A truth that in any case he could not have used, for though the phrase perhaps symbolised a call, it was incapable of creating new powers and making Swann the writer that he was not.'   (*TR*, III: 911)

The revelation is accessible only to those who are predestined by their talents to understand it: Parsifal, the Narrator.

6   The 'transmission' of the Sonata to the Narrator by Odette (*WBG, I: 570–5*)

Swann has married Odette. Their union has produced a daughter, Gilberte, with whom the young Narrator is in love. He gains admittance to the Swanns' house, and 'sometimes, before going to dress, Mme Swann would sit down at the piano'. Thus he is able to listen to the Andante from the Sonata on several occasions.

When the Narrator hears it for the first time, he is in exactly the same position as Swann at the time of the 'archetypal' performance: he hardly distinguishes the phrase that has become so familiar to the Swanns. 'Even when I had heard the sonata from beginning to end, it remained almost wholly invisible to me, like a monument of which distance or a haze allows us to catch but a faint and fragmentary glimpse.' There is a return to the impressionistic atmosphere of the outset. Like Parsifal exposed to the Grail, the Narrator understands nothing. He is sensible only to the charm of Odette. That is why this passage tells us nothing about the Sonata as such, but rather describes at length what happens when we hear a work for the first time; it also offers the beautiful meditation on posterity which has already been discussed (see above, p. 38).

In fact this episode reaffirms for the last time Swann's fundamental incomprehension, thus prolonging the subject matter of 'Swann in love': 'The moment when night is falling among the trees, when the arpeggios of the violin call down a cooling dew upon the earth. You must admit it's lovely; it shows all the static side of moonlight, which is the *essential part*.' Swann cannot separate the little phrase from the circumstances in which he last heard it, before being banished from the Verdurins' salon:

'That's what is expressed so well in that little phrase, the Bois de Boulogne plunged in a cataleptic trance.' I understood from other remarks he made that this nocturnal foliage was simply that beneath whose shade, in many a restaurant on the outskirts of Paris, he had listened on so many evenings to the little phrase. In place of the profound meaning that he had so often sought in it, what it now recalled to Swann were the leafy boughs, ordered, wreathed, painted round about it . . . was the whole of one spring season which he had not been able to enjoy at the time.

For although Swann has not progressed in his understanding of the Sonata since his marriage, he has nevertheless established new associations with the little phrase which have driven out the older ones: 'Vinteuil's phrase now shows me only the things to which I paid no attention then. Of my troubles, my loves of those days, it recalls nothing, it has swapped things around.' And as Proust has the 'knack of the commonplace phrase' when he wants to show the incapacity of people to grasp the essence of things, he allows Swann to make his ultimate statement of 'aesthetic faith' in the following words: 'What the music shows – to me, at least – is not "the triumph of the Will" or "In Tune with the Infinite," but shall we say old Verdurin in his frock coat in the palmhouse in the Zoological Gardens.'

7   The comparison of Vinteuil with Wagner (C, III: 154–9)

It is not until very much later in *A la recherche* that the Narrator next encounters the Sonata. This is because, as Pierre Costil rightly notes, he has to have time to experience jealousy, the intermittencies of the heart, disappointment in love and the ultimate extinction of his love – in short, to cover the same emotional ground with Albertine as Swann has done with Odette – before he is capable of understanding the message of the Septet and the revelation it brings.

Like the 'transmission' scene, this passage tells us little about the Sonata itself, since it is devoted essentially to the comparison with Wagner already discussed in chapter 2 (pp. 12ff.). Nevertheless, if it is considered in relation to the Narrator's evolution and his search for a vocation, its function is clear. From the very first, the Narrator has passed beyond the stage of Swann, where the work and his love are connected: 'I did not even go out of my way to notice how, in the latter [the Sonata], the combination of the sensual and the anxious motifs corresponded more closely now to my love for Albertine'. No, he considers it in relation to his desire to create: 'Approaching the sonata from another point of view, regarding it in itself as the work of a great artist, I was carried back upon the *tide* of sound to the days at Combray – I do not mean Montjouvain and the Méséglise way, but to my walks along the Guermantes way – when I myself had longed to become an artist.' One single word is enough to recall the Sonata's initial association with the sea. As with Swann at the Saint-Euverte soirée, involuntary memory works to the full, but it projects the Narrator not in the direction of sexuality (Montjouvain, i.e. the scene in which Vinteuil's portrait is profaned by the two lesbians, his daughter and her friend, and Méséglise, i.e. Swann and the impasse of his relationship with Odette) but towards art, i.e. the Guermantes Way, where he had enjoyed the experience – temporarily interrupted – of the steeples of Martinville and the trees of Hudimesnil. By referring explicitly to the 'two ways', Proust prepares us for the reunification which will be made possible by the Septet, in other words, the redemption of sexuality through the work of art.

What is the main concern, now, in Proust's aesthetic scheme? To find through the medium of art 'that sensation of individuality for which we seek in vain in our everyday existence'. This individual character has already been acquired by the little phrase: 'It was so peculiarly itself, it had so individual, so irreplaceable a charm . . .' (*S*, I: 231). In this respect it was comparable to a leitmotif from *Tristan* (*S*, I: 381). Consequently it is not surprising that Proust should take his examples of individuation through music from the works of Wagner: 'Music, very different in this respect from Albertine's society, helped me to descend into myself, to discover new things: the variety that I had sought in vain in life, in travel, but a longing for which was none the less renewed in me by this sonorous tide whose sunlit waves now came to expire at my feet.' And Proust cites 'the song of a bird, the ring of a hunter's horn, the air that a shepherd plays upon his pipe' as examples of individual motifs perfectly integrated into the work that accommodates them.

However, in spite of his dithyrambic praise of Wagner, the Narrator is more troubled than convinced by his 'Vulcan-like skill': 'Could it be this that gave to great artists the *illusory aspect* of a fundamental, irreducible originality, apparently the reflexion of a more than human reality, actually the result of *industrious toil*? If art is no more than that, it is no more real than life and I had less cause for regret. I went on playing *Tristan*' − and the passage will end in the most prosaic fashion. However far Wagner might take us towards the absolute, his works still bear traces of the craftsman's bench. Proust does not dare to write that they seem manufactured, but he lets it be understood. This is the significance of the reference to Siegfried's hammer-blows and the substitution of an aeroplane − 'brand-name Mystère' − for Lohengrin's swan: 'However high one flies, one is prevented to some extent from enjoying the silence of space by the overpowering roar of the engine!' Of course the long disquisition on Wagner enables Proust − and this is of crucial importance − to evoke the single, global work of art in which all the motifs intermingle and interrelate with each other. But it is also a stage in the artistic quest. Wagner's skill is redolent of artifice. Veiled self-criticism? Perhaps. But we understand, as a result, that the stages of the quest could not have come about in relation to a real work of art: the absolute work of art can only be an imaginary one, the magical embodiment of the essential, which, although it might display aspects typical of Wagner (cross-reference among the themes, reminiscence of previous works in a new work), can only occur, in the chronology of the quest, *after* the real work that it most closely resembles in its organisation.

8   The Septet (C, III: 250–65)

The revelation is at hand. And it will happen in that same salon of the Verdurins in which Swann had merely projected his own emotions onto the little phrase without managing to interpret correctly the essence he had sensed in it. In fifteen pages the Narrator will relive all of Swann's experience and the beginning of his own; but this time he will bring it to a conclusion.

'In the body of this septet, different elements presented themselves one after another [in order] to combine at the close . . .' The Septet is a unified work, self-contained, complete, with its own internal logic whereby the themes and motifs pursue each other, separate and reunite; in this respect it is a microcosm of *A la recherche* itself. It also represents the final accomplishment of the whole of Vinteuil's undertaking: '[His] sonata and, as I later discovered, his other works as well, had been no more than timid essays, exquisite but very slight, beside the triumphal and consummate masterpiece now being revealed to me.' This is an allusion not only to *A la recherche* but also to the creative development of Proust himself, though the latter could not have been recognised by the reader of 1923: it is only since 1954 that we have known *A la recherche* was preceded by that 'timid essay', or dry run, which was *Jean Santeuil*. Above all, however, the experience that the Narrator derives from his discovery of the Septet is immediately juxtaposed with his experience of love:

I could not help recalling by comparison that, in the same way too, I had thought of the other worlds that Vinteuil had created as being self-enclosed as each of my loves had been; whereas in reality . . . if I now considered not my love for Albertine but my whole life, my other loves too had been no more than slight and timid essays that were paving the way, appeals that were unconsciously clamouring, for this vaster love: my love for Albertine.

Then the Narrator's thoughts fork, giving way to a description of his disappointment in love and of his self-questioning about Albertine: has she or has she not, in fact, been the lover of Mlle Vinteuil's friend? Proust thus prepares for the conjunction of the two great axes of *A la Recherche*: the way in which the amorous experience of the Narrator is poisoned by his doubts about the woman he loves, and the quest for the work of art.

And of course it is the Septet that will enable him to pass beyond the stage of doubt and disappointment: 'Something more mysterious than Albertine's love seemed to be promised at the outset of this work, in those first cries of dawn.' In this way the Narrator relives the experience of Swann, who had also had the intuition of another dimension. As with him, his thoughts are fixed for a moment on Vinteuil. But already it is Vinteuil the artist and not the man who interests him: 'This Vinteuil, whom I had known [to be] so timid and sad, had been capable − when he had to choose a timbre and to blend another with it − of an audacity, and in the full sense of the word a felicity, as to which the hearing of any of his works left one in no doubt.' The work is not, then, in the image of its creator. Turning his thoughts in this direction, the Narrator − unlike Swann − is going to pass easily beyond the biographical stage:

Vinteuil had been dead for many years; but in the sound of these instruments which he had loved, it had been given him to go on living, for an unlimited time, a part at least of his life. Of his life as a man solely? If art was indeed but a prolongation of life, was it worth while to sacrifice anything to it? Was it not as unreal as life itself?[5] The more I listened to this septet, the less I could believe this to be so.

A point of no return has been reached. The doubts that troubled the Narrator in the preceding passage, the reflection on the work of Wagner, are about to disperse. For − let it be stressed again − we have passed from a real work, and one in which creative artifice is still apparent, to an imaginary work which represents the pure, absolute work that escapes every contingency. Proust's thinking is once again remarkably consistent: if he instructed Céleste Albaret to burn his notebooks once he no longer had any need of them, it was surely because *A la recherche* too had to appear to the reader as itself being this work, perfect, self-contained and independent of the conditions (both biographical and technical) in which it was created. The theme of *Contre Sainte-Beuve* thus returns:

For those phrases, historians of music could no doubt find affinities and pedigrees in the works of other great composers, but only for secondary reasons, external resemblances, analogies ingeniously discovered by reasoning rather than felt as the result of a direct impression. The impression conveyed by these Vinteuil phrases was different from any other, as though, in spite of the conclusions to which science seems to point, the individual did exist.

This individual is revealed by the Vinteuil Septet as being literally beyond those contingencies of creation which had irritated the Narrator in the case of Wagner. Let us recall: 'Could it be this [a Vulcan-like skill] that gave to great artists the illusory aspect of a fundamental, irreducible originality, apparently the reflexion of a more than human reality, actually the result of industrious toil?' (C, III: 158–9).

Here the Narrator distinguishes between two types of similarity: 'It was precisely when he [Vinteuil] was striving with all his might to create something new that one recognised, beneath the apparent differences, the profound similarities and the deliberate resemblances that existed in the body of a work'. What a lesson in the art of poetry! Deliberate resemblances are the result of industrious toil; the rest, of the composer's desire to look only towards the future. Here we are touching on an essential point in Proust's aesthetics: the absolute is located beyond the scope of the intellect:

When Vinteuil took up the same phrase again and again, diversified it, amused himself by altering its rhythm, by making it reappear in its original form, those deliberate resemblances, the work of his intellect, *necessarily superficial*, never succeeded in being as striking as the disguised, involuntary resemblances, which broke out in different colours, between the two separate masterpieces; for then Vinteuil, striving to do something new, interrogated himself, with all the power of his creative energy, reached down to his essential self at those depths where, whatever be the question asked, it is in the same accent, that is to say its own, that it replies. Such an accent, the accent of Vinteuil . . .

What is of crucial importance in the Septet, then, is not the effort of will, the 'analytical forms of reasoning', but the specificity that the work displays in relation to all the others at one and the same time as it shares a stylistic relationship with them. The Septet surpasses the Sonata inasmuch as it is something more than a work in which the little phrase reappears. Clearly it is this last feature that makes the most immediate impression on the Narrator: 'This was an unpublished work of Vinteuil in which he had merely amused himself . . . by reintroducing the little phrase for a moment.' An effort of will, in other words. But the Septet is indeed more than this, and that is why the little phrase does not appear subsequently:[6] what matters is 'the accent of Vinteuil', his personal style, which is the fruit of his 'eternal investigations'.

Now, the absolute world of the Sonata belongs to a world that is inaccessible and religious, the world which was revealed to us in detail during the Saint-Euverte performance. As in the preceding passages, Proust intersperses his description with little observations which lend the Septet the same religious atmosphere as the Sonata: the work embodies a 'prayer', a 'speculation . . . in the world of angels', a 'divine round' or 'the mystic hope of the crimson Angel of the Dawn'. This atmosphere contrasts with the falsely religious attitude of Mme Verdurin, who buries her head in her hands as if she were in church.

If the great, profound work comes from anywhere at all, its source certainly cannot be found in biographical contingencies or even in the play of stylistic affinities. It seems to emanate from an invisible and inexpressible beyond.

Because individuality exists through the stylistic unity of a creative artist, works of art tell us much more about the world than all our travels or love affairs ever could. And that is why art is superior to life, for each work of art transmits to us the individual experience of its creator:

The only true voyage of discovery, the only really rejuvenating experience, would be not to visit strange lands but to possess other eyes, to see the universe through the eyes of another, of a hundred others, to see the hundred universes that each of them sees, that each of them is; and this we can do with an Elstir, with a Vinteuil; with men like these we do really fly from star to star.

By the skilful use of a classic Proustian device – the placing of an interval between the Andante and the following movement – the description brings us back to the superficial remarks of the listeners. But only for a moment. This is just a springboard for the next stage of the analysis, which brings us to our final goal, namely the realisation that music is a form of specific language which serves as a model.

Already Proust has shown us the extent to which the fundamental question that Vinteuil poses in his work, a question 'free from analytical forms of reasoning', is inaccessible to ordinary language: 'We can gauge its depth, but no more translate it into human speech than can disembodied spirits when, evoked by a medium, they are questioned by him about the secrets of death . . . Each artist seems thus to be the native of an unknown country, which he himself has forgotten'. Yet Proust goes further in his formulation, in what seems to me to be the decisive passage in the whole of *A la recherche* as far as the relationship between music and literature is concerned:

I wondered whether music might not be the unique example of what might have been – if the invention of language, the formation of words, the analysis of ideas had not intervened – the means of communication between souls. It is like a possibility that has come to nothing; humanity has developed along other lines, those of spoken and written language.

From being the descriptive medium of the Saint-Euverte soirée, Proust's form of musical semiology has become metaphysical.

Proust now resumes his description of the performance: phrases from the Sonata recur in the Septet, 'as things recur in life'. 'This phrase was what might have seemed most eloquently to characterise . . . those impressions which at remote intervals I experienced in my life as starting-points, foundation-stones for the construction of a *true life*'. These last two words anticipate the famous formulation in *Time Regained*: 'Real life, life at last laid bare and illuminated – the only life in consequence which can be said to be really lived – is literature' (*TR*, III: 931). Above all, however, music imitates life, and foreshadows the effort the Narrator must make in order to gather the scraps of life together into a single, organised whole, because it works like involuntary memory: a fresh occurrence of a theme already heard recalls its first appearance to us, just as the paving-stones in the courtyard will later recall the episode of the madeleine.

And so it is the play of musical phrases that brings the Narrator back to his fundamental problem: will he be capable of producing a literary work of comparable depth? That 'ineffable joy which seemed to come from paradise . . . would it ever be attainable to me?' The musical work that is the Septet – the work that has become, for the Narrator, a model for the literary work still to be written – is also the one that tells him to set to work: in the joyous theme that rings out at the beginning and at the end of the Septet, the Narrator hears a call to create and to embark resolutely upon his true vocation.

*

This perception of the absolute does not come to the Narrator as soon as he hears the beginning of the Septet. In fact, if we isolate from the passage the description of the work itself, we see that the latter is divided clearly into two parts.

In the first, we no longer find the description of those qualities of sound which characterised initial perception at the time of the 'archetypal' performance and which are still present in the first evocations of the little phrase. On the other hand the sea atmosphere of these early appearances returns in force, in the form of precise, concrete observations.

'It was upon flat, unbroken surfaces like those of the sea on a morning that threatens storm, in the midst of an eerie silence, in an infinite void, that this new work began, and it was into a rose-red daybreak that this unknown universe was drawn from the silence and the night to build up gradually before me.' It is dawn; a louder phrase, like 'a mystical cock-crow', evokes 'the ineffable but ear-piercing call of eternal morning'. Then the work becomes more violent: 'The atmosphere, cold, rain-washed, electric . . . changed continually, eclipsing the crimson promise of the dawn.' A new, joyous motif is about to appear: 'At noon, however, in a burst of scorching but transitory sunlight, it [the atmosphere] seemed to reach fulfilment in a heavy, rustic, almost cloddish gaiety in which the lurching, riotous clangour of bells . . . seemed the material representation of the coarsest joy.' When Proust evokes the work in the passage that follows, he takes up the same characteristics again: the 'first cries of dawn', 'the still inert crimson of the morning sky above the sea'.

It is difficult to read this description without thinking of Debussy's *La Mer*, most particularly because of the programmatic title of the latter's first movement: 'De l'aube à midi sur la mer' ('From dawn to noon on the sea'). If we bothered with point-by-point comparisons between the musical model to which Proust here seems explicitly to refer and the description he gives, we would note the dawn-like atmosphere of the opening, the call theme and the joyous motif which the Narrator specifically dislikes. But obviously it is not the resemblance to a specific work that concerns us here: it is the fact that the Septet is compared, in this first phase, to a work that is frankly descriptive and whose impressionistic character corresponds to the vague and fragmentary nature of our perception of the beginning of a work. The Debussian atmosphere seems the important thing to note about this first phase of the Septet, just as we have noted it at the start of the 'archetypal' performance. And in accordance with a method already discussed (p. 42), another, much earlier passage in *A la recherche* confirms our analysis: 'We could just make out, barely distinguishable from the luminous azure, *rising out of the water, rose-pink*, silvery, faint, *the little bells* that were sounding the Angelus round about Féterne. "That is rather *Pelléas*, too," I suggested to Mme de Cambremer-Legrandin. "You know the scene I mean" ' (*CP*, II: 851). The textual analogy is unmistakable and confirms the reference to Debussy.

During the course of the passage devoted to the Septet, the Sonata retrospectively acquires new descriptive elements. These elements do not change its basic character but reinforce certain aspects which have already been encountered: we observe, above all, that 'the sonata opened upon a lily-white pastoral dawn', in which 'honeysuckles' mixed with 'white geraniums' – a feature which explains both its colour (the 'White Sonata', as opposed to the crimson of the Septet) and its 'virginal, plant-strewn world'. To be sure, the Sonata of 'Swann in love' already evoked the world of plants, especially through the sense of smell, but the reinforcement here of the plant theme is very clear. I shall later put forward a theory in order to explain it.

In the second phase of its development, the Septet leaves the descriptive world of the seascape in order to engage in the more fundamental play of purely musical questions and answers, one in which concrete words have disappeared. For in the Septet, Proust tells us, 'the questioning phrases had become more pressing, more unquiet' by comparison with the Sonata, 'the answers more mysterious; the washed-out air of morning and evening seemed to affect the very strings of the instruments.' From this transitional sentence onwards we are concerned only with transformations of the phrase, the appearance of the second motif and the struggle that ensues between them: 'If these creatures [the two motifs] confronted one another, *they did so stripped of their physical bodies, of their appearance, of their names*, finding in me an inward spectator – himself indifferent, too, to names and particulars – to appreciate *their immaterial and dynamic combat* and follow passionately *its sonorous vicissitudes*.' Nothing could be clearer: we are concerned no longer with descriptive scene-painting but with a purely musical argument in which external factors have been erased.

It is worth looking at the context of what I have just called the transi-

tional sentence, for I think it provides the key to the connection between the musical profundity that has been evoked and the literary
work that has still to be written. Let us examine the whole passage:

Each artist seems thus to be the native of an unknown country, which he
himself has forgotten, and which is different from that whence another great
artist, setting sail for the earth, will eventually emerge. Certain it was that
Vinteuil, in his latest works, seemed to have drawn nearer to that unknown
country. The atmosphere was no longer the same as in the sonata, *the questioning phrases had become more pressing*, more unquiet, the answers more
mysterious; the washed-out air of morning and evening seemed to affect the
very *strings* of the instruments. Marvellously though Morel played, *the sounds
that came from his violin seemed to me singularly piercing, almost shrill. This harshness* was pleasing, and, as in certain voices, one felt in it *a sort of moral quality
and intellectual superiority.* . . . the more intelligent section of the public is not
misled, since *Vinteuil's last compositions were ultimately declared to be his most
profound.* And yet no programme, no subject matter, supplied any intellectual
basis for judgment. One simply sensed that it was a question of *the transposition
of creative profundity into terms of sound.*

I have italicised those phrases in the text which, if taken individually,
would hardly be sufficient to call to mind the quartets of Beethoven but
which, when gathered together in the same paragraph, suggest them
unmistakably to the musician. Although the Septet involves piano,
harp, flute and oboe, Proust here talks only of strings. Anyone who has
heard Beethoven's late quartets will find the words 'piercing', 'shrill'
and 'harshness' highly pertinent (see Piroué 1960: 182). Posterity's
judgment on the profundity of the quartets is absolutely identical to
what we are told here about the last works of Vinteuil. Besides, Proust
has already referred to Beethoven's quartets in his novel, and not just
in any old fashion. In *Within a Budding Grove* the Twelfth, Thirteenth,
Fourteenth and Fifteenth Quartets are explicitly cited as examples of
works which, like *A la recherche* itself, needed time to create their own
posterity on account of their novelty (*WBG*, I: 564). Above all,
however, a philological detail seems to bear out the consistency of this
general impression. The reference to 'questioning phrases' that 'press'
reminds one irresistibly of the epigraph to the last movement of the
Sixteenth Quartet, 'Der schwer gefasste Entschluss' (see Example 1).
This epigraph provides the material for several statements in stretto
before giving way to the reply (see Example 2).

Ex. 1
Grave

Muss   es   sein?

Ex. 2
Allegro

Es   muss   sein!   Es   muss   sein!

Surely it is the last movement in its entirety that is depicted in the
physical struggle between the two motifs. Proust knew the late
Beethoven quartets well, having heard them performed by the Capet
Quartet at the Salle Pleyel, on 26 February 1913 among other occasions, and also having had them played for him at his home by the
Poulet Quartet in the spring of 1916 (furthermore, this epigraph is
quoted by Lavignac on p. 504 of his *Voyage artistique à Bayreuth*,
which, as I have shown above, was the source of Proust's information
about the supposed prior composition of the 'Good Friday Spell').
Now, we cannot fail to spot the link between the text of the epigraph
and the very subject of *A la recherche*. This is the translation: 'The
resolution made with difficulty. Must it be? It must be! It must be!'
These three sentences sum up all the Narrator's uncertainty with
regard to his vocation.

   There is an obvious objection to this apparent link between the finale
of the Sixteenth Quartet and the last movement of the Septet, namely
that when Proust refers explicitly to the Beethoven quartets in *Within
a Budding Grove* he talks of the Twelfth to Fifteenth Quartets but not
the Sixteenth. Moreover, when Proust displays a particular enthusiasm
for the quartets in his correspondence it is the finale of the Fifteenth
that is at issue. Thus in a letter to Curtius, quoted by Benoist-Méchin
(1957: 21), he evokes the 'sublime theme of the finale of the Fifteenth
Quartet, which emits such a powerful human tenderness that one cannot listen to it without feeling one's heart expand'. In his preface to
Morand's *Tendres Stocks*, dated 15 November 1920, Proust is still talking of 'the pre-Mendelssohnian (or rather the infinitely super-

Mendelssohnian) phrase of the Fifteenth Quartet' (in *CSB*: 616). And in the novel, M. de Charlus reproaches Morel for playing a piano transcription of the Fifteenth Quartet (*CP*, II: 1042–3).

I shall make three points in this connection. In the first place, these three sole written references that have come down to us are not a sufficient basis for asserting that the finale of the Fifteenth Quartet was more important to Proust than that of the Sixteenth. Secondly, we cannot rule out the possibility that there was some confusion between the Fifteenth and Sixteenth Quartets in Proust's mind. After all, we have seen that he was capable of confusing the second and third acts of *Parsifal*. On the one hand, Proust had heard the Fifteenth and Sixteenth Quartets in a Capet concert of February 1913 (*NE*, I: 1378). On the other, in a letter to Montesquiou he describes the finale of the Fifteenth Quartet as expressing the 'delirium of a sick man who was to die shortly afterwards'. Proust is mistaken here: the Fifteenth Quartet was written in 1825; it was with the Sixteenth, written in 1826, that Beethoven concluded his life's work (he died on 26 March 1827).[7] Finally, knowing the care with which Proust systematically concealed his sources, I venture the following hypothesis. As Costil has shown (1958–9), Proust wrote the 'transmission' scene in order to provide a link with the description of the Septet. Was it not precisely because, in so doing, he had the idea of using the Sixteenth Quartet in connection with the Vinteuil that he deliberately omitted to mention it when he came to describe the Septet itself? Moreover, there is another allusion in *A la recherche*, similarly without a precise reference, to the questioning phrases that are so characteristic of the Beethoven finale: 'Thus, every other minute, the same question seemed to be put to Jupien intently in M. de Charlus's ogling, like those questioning phrases of Beethoven's, indefinitely repeated at regular intervals and intended – with an exaggerated lavishness of preparation – to introduce a new theme, a change of key, a "re-entry" ' (*CP*, II: 627). Listen to this finale: nothing could describe it better.

Yet it is another quotation from *A la recherche* that tends to confirm the link between a phrase of Beethoven and the very subject of the novel:

But let us bear in mind, rather, the countless writers who, dissatisfied with the passage they have just written, read some eulogy of the genius of Chateaubriand, or evoke the spirit of some great artist whose equal they aspire to be, humming to themselves, for instance, *a phrase of Beethoven* the melancholy of which they compare with *what they have been trying to express in their prose,* and become so imbued with this idea of genius that they add it to their own productions when they return to them, no longer see them in the light in which they appeared at first, and, hazarding an act of faith in the value of their work, say to themselves: 'After all!' without taking into account that, into the total which determines their ultimate satisfaction, they have introduced the memory of marvellous pages of Chateaubriand which they assimilate to their own but which, after all, they did not write.   (*WBG*, I: 518–19)

Thus the allusion to 'Muss es sein?' from the *last* movement of Beethoven's *last* quartet – a veritable cryptogram – would seem to combine the decision to undertake the great work to which the Narrator is led by the Septet with the idea of the essential, profound and absolute work of which only music that has passed beyond descriptive and quasi-linguistic contingencies can provide us with an image.

*

At this decisive point in *A la recherche*, the passage on the Septet opens up a fundamental conjunction which will find its final resolution in *Time Regained*. The Septet is not only, in its relation to the Sonata, the image of the work of art through which we distract ourselves from our failures in love. Nor is it only the model that the Narrator must pursue. It also represents the point at which the Guermantes Way may meet the Méséglise Way. For while the Narrator experiences in the presence of the Septet the same impression that he felt on seeing the steeples of Martinville (see *S*, I: 196–8) and the trees of Hudimesnil (*WBG*, I: 770–3) – when he had experienced the first, short-lived joys of literary creation – and while both of these places are located on the Guermantes Way,[8] the Septet is also the product of the Méséglise Way (or Swann's Way), where Mlle Vinteuil and her friend sadistically profaned her father's portrait at Montjouvain (see *S*, I: 173–80). What are we to understand from the end of the passage on the Septet? That, to make amends, Mlle Vinteuil's friend has spent several years working on the composer's manuscripts so that the Septet might be granted access to an existence which reunites the scraps of sketch in a single, complete work: '[Mlle Vinteuil's friend] had the consolation of ensuring an immortal and compensatory glory for the composer over whose last years she had cast such a shadow.' Thus the Septet is a work of redemption, through which the two ways, brought together at last, and homosexual love, at last redeemed, permit the Narrator to hear the joyous phrase that is characteristic of the Septet:

It was thanks to her, in compensation, that I had been able to apprehend the strange summons which I should henceforth never cease to hear, as the promise and proof that there existed something other, realisable no doubt through art, than the nullity that I had found in all my pleasures and in love itself, and that if my life seemed to me so futile, at least it had not yet accomplished everything.

Now, musically we have already heard this joyous summons before: in the passage identified with Debussy (the joyous motif at the start); in Wagner – the joyous melody of the shepherd in *Tristan*, announcing the return of Isolde and assimilated by Proust to the creative joy of the composer (*C*, III: 158); and even here, at this climactic point, behind which the profile of Beethoven may be glimpsed. *In this order*, the three composers who underpin the Sonata and the Septet also reproduce the three stages of the summons to creation that is now heard; and they do so through the clarion call which is at first barely understood, then given the more specific status of a leitmotif and finally made the essential matter of the great, profound work.

By way of conclusion Proust returns to his initial theme. In the work of Vinteuil, the Septet transcends all that has preceded it: 'Compared with this septet, certain phrases from the Sonata which were all that the public knew appeared so commonplace that it was difficult to understand how they could have aroused so much admiration.' This provides the cue for a last reference to Wagner, which brings the passage to an end: of what value are the famous arias from *Tannhäuser* in comparison with *Tristan, Die Meistersinger* and *The Ring*? Quite simply, they have prepared the way for the masterpieces that we love and whose beauties we could only have guessed at if his work on them had been interrupted prematurely by death – as with Vinteuil, and as with Proust.

*

In several respects, then, the Septet can be seen as a microcosm of *A la recherche* (see above, pp. 59ff.). The very choice of musical ensemble – seven instruments – has never ceased to intrigue commentators. It has been interpreted, rightly, as an allusion to the seven colours and to the seven notes of the scale, and therefore as a mythological symbol of perfection (Matoré and Mecz 1972: 169). The composition of the group has caused surprise: piano, harp, flute, oboe, violin, cello (confused with double bass) and perhaps brass[9] in the plural – this would exceed the number seven. Since Proust was not exactly uncultured musically, he would surely have corrected these inconsistencies if he had had time to reread his manuscript at leisure. But we have probably been wrong in the past to be surprised by the fact that the instrumentation does not correspond to any classical ensemble. Any musician will observe that, with the exception of percussion, all the instrumental *families* (woodwind – flute, oboe; brass; bowed strings – violin, cello; plucked strings – harp; strings that are struck – piano) are represented; and one cannot but see in this another symbol of completeness.

In his article on 'imaginary works of art in Proust', Butor has put forward the daring idea that a correspondence could be established between the number of instruments, the colours of the spectrum, the notes of the scale, the number of transformations undergone by the works of Vinteuil[10] and the number of books in *A la recherche* (1971: 180–1). While the colours and the notes present no problem, the number of transformations should be treated with caution, since Butor is obliged to introduce a 'Verdurin Quartet' which is never described, and which is referred to only in certain versions of the manuscript, in place of 'Sextet' or 'Septet'. It is with regard to this vacillation between the three ensembles that Butor presents his most surprising, but also his most persuasive, argument: 'A study of the manuscripts shows that the transformation of the Sonata into the Septet took place in stages corresponding to the evolution of *A la recherche du temps perdu* itself' (1971: 180). Since this article was written in 1963, it could not take advantage of later research into the genesis of *A la recherche*. In my view this later work does not contradict Butor's hypothesis.

When Proust completed 'Swann in love' in 1912, his initial plan for what was then called *The Intermittencies of the Heart* comprised two parts: 'Time Lost' and 'Time Regained' – an arrangement which corresponded to the initial ensemble of two instruments, namely violin and piano. And when – in 1914, according to Bonnet – Proust decided to replace the 'Good Friday Spell' with an expansion of the Sonata into a quartet, he knew that the two further volumes publicised on the back of the (1914) Grasset edition of *Swann's Way* – *The Guermantes*

Way and *Time Regained* – would, with the appearance of *Within a Budding Grove*, bring the total to four. I believe we can accept Butor's version of what happens later: the Quintet corresponds to the stage announced at the end of 1918, with five volumes (*Cities of the Plain* interpolated). The number of books conceived between 1919 and 1922 grows to six or seven (cf. above, p. 21). As for the 'Sextet' title, Butor invokes the cover of Cahier VIII (Cahier 56 of the B.N.), where we find the words: 'Herewith begins the fifth and last volume of *A la recherche du temps perdu*. This volume is entitled: "Cities of the Plain III – Time Regained" ' – 'a subtitle', Butor comments, 'which was later cancelled in order to be reserved as the title of a sixth and final volume' (1971: 180–1).

Yoshikawa, in his meticulous study of the genesis of the Vinteuil Septet, has expressed reservations about this interpretation: 'The first complete version of the manuscript (in which the Septet and Sextet occur) was finished by 1918 at the latest, when Proust was still thinking of five volumes in all' (1979: 315). Perhaps, but as Yoshikawa himself says earlier, 'It would be useful to go through the fair copy of the manuscript, differentiating between the various layers of composition, that is, the main text (on the lines) and the marginal additions.' He also writes, a little further on, 'As far as Proust's vacillations between Septet and Sextet are concerned, we cannot know which conforms the more closely to his final intentions' (*ibid*.: 314–15), but it is hard to accept this particular conclusion, given the image of perfect completeness represented by the number seven.

This debate is of a twofold interest. From the viewpoint of poietic research – for the genesis of *A la recherche* is fascinating in itself – we could reverse the perspective and take Butor's hypothesis as a starting-point for trying to date the marginal additions in the fair copy. From the philological viewpoint, on the other hand, it would be legitimate, if Butor is right, to substitute the word 'septet' for the words 'quartet' and 'sextet' wherever they occur in the Pléiade edition, including (and this would be bound to shock certain Proustians) the very beginning of the novel, in a particularly significant sentence: 'It seemed to me that I myself was the immediate subject of my book: a church, a *quartet*, the rivalry between François I and Charles V' (*S*, I: 3).[11] For it seems established – turning now to the meaning of the book – that the Vinteuil Septet symbolises the work that is to be created: as far as the

Narrator is concerned, it is certainly the redemptive image of an imaginary work written in a Utopian language which, like music, might succeed in transcending human language — and it is surely for this reason that this entire aesthetic (which is also an imaginary one) is that of a novel.

9 The sessions on the pianola (C, III: 378–90)

The Narrator has one more stage to pass through, in what I should like to call the scene of the transmission from music to literature. This passage is not so extended as that describing the performance of the Septet: its purpose is to come to a conclusion.

Proust takes up again the two essential themes of the preceding passage: the unity of Vinteuil's work and the superiority of musical language. The Narrator asks Albertine to play him 'something of Vinteuil' on the pianola:

This music seemed to me *something truer than all known books*. At moments I thought that this was due to the fact that, what we feel about life not being felt in the form of ideas, its literary, that is to say intellectual expression describes it, explains it, analyses it, but does not recompose it as does music, in which the sounds seem to follow the very movement of our being, to reproduce that extreme inner point of our sensations which is the part that gives us that peculiar exhilaration which we experience from time to time.

Weaving together the threads of the preceding passage, Proust compares once again the impression he experiences on hearing a phrase of Vinteuil with what he has felt in the past when in the presence of the steeples of Martinville and the trees of Balbec; he adds a reference to the experience of the madeleine.

The theme of the superiority of musical language is intimately bound up with that of the unity of the work, for the resemblances between similar musical phrases in different works and the similarities between different phrases in one and the same work constitute, as I have already stressed, a musical metaphor for the workings of involuntary memory. Now, these workings are at the root of the recurrence of the themes that lend unity not only to a particular work but also to the entire output of a composer or writer. This is also the essential theme of *A la recherche*, since it is involuntary memory that, at the very end, allows lost time to be regained:

Perhaps it was in this, I said to Albertine, this unknown quality of a unique world which no other composer had ever yet revealed, that the most authentic proof of genius lies, even more than in the content of the work itself. 'Even in literature?' Albertine inquired. 'Even in literature.' And thinking again of the sameness of Vinteuil's works, I explained to Albertine that the great men of letters have never created more than a single work, or rather have never done more than refract through various media an identical beauty which they bring into the world. 'If it were not so late, my sweet,' I said to her, 'I would show you this quality in all the writers whose works you read while I'm asleep, I would show you the same identity as in Vinteuil.'

And the Narrator goes on to demonstrate to Albertine how all the novels of a single writer can be 'superimposed upon one another', just as the Vinteuil Sonata can be superimposed upon *Tristan*, and as is also the case with each of the operas of Wagner and the seven books that make up *A la recherche*.

The transmission from music to literature has indeed taken place. At first, Albertine has played on the pianola 'something of Vinteuil', without the music being specified any further. Proust has reached a level of generality where he no longer needs to name, let alone describe, any particular work. For once the two themes of the preceding passage have been recalled and emphasised through the reference to Vinteuil, it is, above all, particular works of literature that the Narrator discusses with Albertine.

And yet the evocation of Vinteuil that has afforded the Narrator all the elements of the final revelation ends with suspension points rather than a perfect cadence. If we read a little further, we find:

I began to doubt again; I told myself that after all it might be the case that, if Vinteuil's phrases seemed to be the expression of certain states of soul analogous to that which I had experienced when I tasted the madeleine soaked in tea, there was nothing to assure me that the vagueness of such states was a sign of their profundity rather than of our not having yet learned to analyse them, so that there might be nothing more real in them than in other states.

We have to wait another two novels before the episode of the uneven paving-stones in the courtyard finally confirms both the reality of the true life through literature and the literary vocation to which the Narrator would be justified in devoting the rest of his days. Perhaps, through this final hesitation about Vinteuil, Proust intends us to realise that it is by no means certain that the novel the Narrator has written – if it is the one *we* are reading – has succeeded in touching the absolute.

If it *is* indeed the work we are reading, which is not at all certain. For does not the fictional account offered to us tell of the creation of a total, complete and self-contained work of art which attains the sublime and makes palpable the feeling of profundity? In such a work the contingencies of creation, the dross of the writer's craft and its artifices, would no longer rise to the surface of the text. Moreover, the pure and absolute work of art would no longer have even a subject. It would be – as Swann felt of the little phrase – *sine materia*. Another writer, a contemporary of Proust, solved the problem by surrendering to the giddiness of the blank page, that is, by suggesting a subject for a book which remained no more than the Idea of a Book. Yet I prefer Proust's solution to Mallarmé's, even if, in the work of the former, the truth of music exposes literature as a lie or at least emphasises its Utopian aspect. For him, music was particularly well suited to this role.

There can be no doubt that Proust was expressing in his novel a profound personal conviction regarding the metaphysical and semiological status of music. He had already expressed such a conviction in a letter of 20 May 1895 to Suzette Lemaire, in terms which seem to sum up what I have analysed above:

The essence of music is to awake in us a mysterious depth of soul (one which cannot be expressed in literature or in any of the other finite modes of expression that make use of words, and consequently of ideas, that is, things that are determined, or else make use of objects that are determined – painting, sculpture), a depth which begins where finite things, and all the arts that have finite things as their object, end, and where science ends – and which may thereby be called religious.   (*Correspondance*, vol. 1, pp. 388–9)

For Proust, music is the vehicle not of concepts but of musical ideas. It is a disembodied language which speaks without specifying, a language capable of expressing the inexpressible; it unfolds in time while at the same time escaping from time; it is an essence in its pure state. Later, in our own day, Lévi-Strauss will provide the most radical extension of the Proustian investigation: music, for him, like myth, is a machine for eliminating time (1969: 16).

*

*   *

My explicit references to the music known to Proust are not, therefore, gratuitous. *A la recherche* displays a veritable syntax of allusion which makes any reading of it at once fascinating, difficult and infinite. Proust's musical allusions constitute no more than a pinhead in the entire allusive system of *A la recherche*, but a pinhead of fundamental importance; and it is their meaning in relation to the novel's particular subject – our relationship with Time – that must now be clarified.

We have seen how the quest for an absolute musical language began with the dim perception of a music which was pure and very vaguely descriptive; then how an effort of the intellect allowed indefinite contours to become more precise, descriptive music to compete with painting and musical phrases to turn into actual ideas, until music could finally be apprehended in its purity, profundity and transcendence. In the course of this progression, which corresponds at the same time to the stages of musical perception – from the vague to the distinct, culminating in essence and truth – we have traced a path backwards from Debussy to Wagner and ultimately to Beethoven (cf. p. 70). One cannot fail to observe that the hierarchy thus established by Proust, whether it corresponds to his deepest tastes or to the necessities of his 'demonstration', turns the progress of history on its head, just as the workings of memory enable us to know the true life; it is as if the essence could only be apprehended once time had been turned back, abolished, annulled, 'in the one and only medium in which it [the being within me] could exist and enjoy the essence of things, that is to say: outside time' (*TR*, III: 904). Another passage from *Time Regained* is clear on this matter: 'Our vanity, our passions, our spirit of imitation, our abstract intellect,* our habits have long been at work, and it is the task of art to undo this work of theirs, *making us travel back in the direction from which we have come* to the depths where what has really existed lies unknown within us' (*TR*, III: 932). It is interesting to compare this backward progression at which we have arrived through our analysis with a particularly remarkable passage in which Mme de Cambremer notes an affinity between Wagner and Debussy:

Because she considered herself 'advanced,' because (in matters of art only) 'one could never be far enough to the Left,' she maintained not merely that music

---

* 'Intelligence' in Scott Moncrieff/Kilmartin. [Trans.]

progressed, but that it progressed along a single straight line, and that Debussy was in a sense a super-Wagner, slightly more advanced again than Wagner.

(*CP*, II: 843)

The Narrator timidly disputes her contention:

She did not realise that if Debussy was not as independent of Wagner as she herself was to suppose in a few years' time, because an artist will after all make use of the weapons he has captured to free himself finally from one whom he has momentarily defeated, he nevertheless sought, when people were beginning to feel surfeited with works that were too complete, in which everything was expressed, to satisfy an opposite need.   (*Ibid.*)

Proust reminds us that art does not 'progress' in a straight line, but that each new school or tendency arises in reaction to the preceding one, even if it is only with the passage of time that we see, much later, what the two apparently contrasting composers have in common. Here we must note Proust's perspicacity, not only in relation to this mini-theory of the history of the arts but also with respect to musical criticism. There is less merit today in recognising what *Pelléas* owes to the endless melody, the leitmotif technique and, in certain passages, the style of *Parsifal*. But in presenting this idea Proust kills two birds with one stone: at the same time as he refuses to place Debussy at the top of the hierarchy which would locate him chronologically after Beethoven and Wagner, he also shows why Debussy should be associated with the beginning and not the end of the Septet. Three sorts of temporality, then, emerge from these comparisons: the naive temporality of the snobs, who believe in the linear progress of art; the more real, more uncertain temporality of the life enjoyed by works of art in relation to their public; and the backward journey through time whereby all temporality is abolished. Only the last leads to the epiphany of Truth.

Proust's aesthetic and metaphysical conception of music is too consistent for us not to look for a source. I think we may be able to find it in Schopenhauer.

4

From Vinteuil to Schopenhauer

As I indicated in the Introduction, it is to Anne Henry, after Beckett, that we owe the idea of addressing the musical episodes in Proust from the perspective of Schopenhauer: 'The only score analysed here by Proust is that of Schopenhauer, to which he adds all his personal variations' (1981: 302–3). Henry demonstrates whxt Proust's conception of music owes to German philosophy, first with resi ect to an article of 1894, 'Un Dimanche au Conservatoire' (*ibid*.: 46–55), and then with respect to *A la recherche* (*ibid*.: 301–7). Discussing the former, she criticises interpretations of Schopenhauer that she considers too liberal and praises the perceptiveness of Proust; 'Able to restore to Schopenhauer his true intention, he finds that art is singled out in his work as the supreme activity . . .' (*ibid*.: 47). She shows that Proust assigns to music the most elevated place in his hierarchy of the arts, just as is the case in *The World as Will and Idea*: for Schopenhauer, all the arts except music are bound up with mimesis; also, music can 'express through its configurations all the essence of the Will — that is, of feeling — [and] provide, without going through the medium of ideas, a dynamic and diversified analogue of that which is itself dynamic and diversified' (*ibid*.: 50). Then, moving on to *A la recherche*, Henry notes that music appears ast, after architecture, sculpture and painting, as in treatises of aesthetics (*ibid*.: 281); she cites several examples to show how Proust has literally paraphrased Schopenhauer's text, in particular with regard to the capacity of music to reach the innermost essence of things (*ibid*.: 303). Then she goes over again, in general terms, the ground covered by Swann and the Narrator in the passages I have examined above (*ibid*.: 303–7).

Anne Henry has opened up a crucial avenue of research which I want to pursue by exploring in further detail the themes analysed in chapter 3. I shall try to relate these themes to *The World as Will and Idea*, in terms both of its general structure and of certain specific details.

On reading the *World* we are immediately struck by the similarity of viewpoint between the two writers on the basic objectives of their respective books. Let us begin with time, which runs through the *World* like a leitmotif and from which only contemplation of the essence allows us to escape. Schopenhauer definitely conceived his work as a means of salvation and redemption for the *pauci homines* who would understand its message: 'From such knowledge [pure contemplation] we get philosophy as well as art; in fact, we shall find in this book that we can also reach that disposition of mind which alone leads to true holiness and to salvation from the world' (1958, I: 274). The author was aware that his work would require time to find its readership, and his remarks about posterity in the preface to the second edition recall irresistibly those pages on the same subject from *Within a Budding Grove* which I have discussed: 'Everything of value needs a long time to gain authority' (1958, I: xviii). So it is not surprising that the philosopher should describe his redemptive work in terms which, *mutatis mutandis*, could be applied to *A la recherche*:

Since, as I have said, this whole work is only the unfolding of a single thought, it follows therefrom that all its parts have the most intimate connexion with one another. Not only does each part stand in a necessary relation to that which immediately precedes it, and thus presuppose it as within the reader's memory, as is the case with all philosophies consisting merely of a series of inferences, *but every part of the whole work is related to every other part, and presupposes it.*[1] For this reason, it is required that the reader should remember not only what has just been said, but also every previous remark, so that he is able to connect it with what he is reading at any moment, however much else there may have been between the two. (1958, I: 285–6)

Schopenhauer's book is based on two all-important premises: the world is my idea; the world is my will. The world is my idea: that is to say, there is no perception of the external world that does not depend upon my body, my mood, my ego; all knowledge is at one remove. The world is my will: that is to say, we act as if we were pursuing an end, but this action is instinctive, and in reality without any teleological aspect. Accordingly, 'the intellect is only the product and instrument of the will. This theory can be summed up in the following words of a character in Emile Zola (*Le Docteur Pascal*): "That is the crucial point. There is no other will in the world than that force which impels everything to life, to a life more and more developed and superior" ' (Dietrich, in Schopenhauer 1909: 5). Further, the will objectifies itself in phenomena: it is a unique entity, located outside time. Consequently it is accessible only through ideas.

Schopenhauer makes a clear distinction between intuition and the intellect. It is through the former that we have immediate access to the essence of things. The latter constructs an idea of the world through the rational intermediaries of concepts and science. He does not denigrate science; he simply considers that it is incapable of grasping things-in-themselves. Nor, for all that, is the role of the intellect negative, for if art and philosophy can put us in contact with the essential world, that is, the Will, artistic and philosophical endeavour presupposes the active intervention of the intellect. It is, indeed, thanks to the intellect that man can destroy the Will-to-Live, embark upon renunciation and achieve holiness.

We can already see what Proust owes to this general scheme. Swann, when he listens to the Sonata, constantly has the intuition that it contains a mysterious essence, but he only seeks to understand it through the medium of the rational intellect. The images he constructs in order to appropriate it are described by Proust as 'substitutes' or 'facsimiles': there can be no better translation, in literary terms, of the philosophical abstraction of the mediating idea beyond which we have to pass. Indeed, I believe it is necessarily in accordance with Schopenhauerian concepts that we must interpret the spirit of *Contre Sainte-Beuve* as found again in *A la recherche*, notably in Swann's attempts to rediscover Vinteuil the man behind his works. Schopenhauer reproaches science for being an etiology, an attempt to provide causal explanations, in other words something closely bound up with time (see his Second Book, chapter 17 [1958, I: 95–9]). Proust, like Schopenhauer, rejects explanations of this type because they divert us from our fundamental quest – which is to look for the essence beyond phenomena.

Swann has this essence within his grasp; for, as Schopenhauer points out, whereas science deals only with phenomenal fragments (1958, I: 351, for example), the essence, i.e. the Will, since it *is* an essence, is present in each fragment (*ibid.*, I: 110ff., 139) – in the little phrase, in the Andante. Consequently Swann is all the more to be blamed for making the little phrase the 'national anthem' of his love for Odette, since this simple musical segment would itself suffice to lead him to the superior world of the essence.

But Swann is only a critic; indeed, he cannot bring his work to a conclusion. And he is a critic of painting at that. Now, in Schopenhauer, as in *A la recherche*, there is a hierarchy of the arts which corresponds to the different levels at which the Will objectifies itself. First of all — for our philosopher — comes the world of minerals, of raw material, which is also the world of architecture. Even at this most basic level, however, there is the presence of beauty, of the essence. If we reread Schopenhauer we can almost hear Proust's voice: 'All these [inorganic, formless things, and even all artifacts] reveal the Ideas through which the will objectif es itself at the lowest levels; they sound, as it were, the deepest, lingering bass-notes of nature. *Gravity, rigidity, fluidity, light*, and so on, are the Ideas that express themselves in rocks, buildings, and masses of water' (1958, I: 210). Consequently it is not surprising that the Sonata, when heard for the very first time, should bathe in a marine world, or that the Septet, before rising to the level of pure music, should evoke the sea. This is because the tripartite evolution of Vinteuil's works that I have elucidated in my analysis follows rigorously the Schopenhauerian journey through the levels of objectivity of the Will.[2] For after the world of inert matter, Schopenhauer invokes the kingdom of plants and — in his hierarchy of the arts — the art of gardening. Let us be in no doubt: it is for this reason that the Sonata has a pastoral, rural character, which will be emphasised during the description of the Septet, thus taking the whole progression back to its source. And if Swann associates the Sonata with the 'Bois de Boulogne plunged in a cataleptic trance' (see above, p. 56), is it not because he is unable to rise beyond the primary, plant world? From this perspective the Sonata — seen in the context of the overall progression of *A la recherche* — must even be linked with the mystery of the hawthorns, which Proust specifically compares with that of music: 'They went on offering me the same charm in inexhaustible profusion, but without letting me delve any more deeply, like those melodies which one can play a hundred times in succession without coming any nearer to their secret' (*S*, I: 151). Besides, it was with the hawthorns that Proust, in one of the early drafts for *Time Regained*, had very clearly associated the quartet that would later become the Septet:

Just as once, at Combray, when having exhausted the joys that the hawthorn afforded me and not wishing to demand them of another flower, I saw a source of new joys spring up for me in the form of a bush of pink thorn on the path leading up from Tansonville, so also, finding no new joy to espouse[3] in the Vinteuil Sonata, I suddenly felt, on hearing the quartet, that I would experience that joy again, the very same and yet still virginal, enveloping and revealing to my sight another world, similar but unknown.   (*MPG*: 293)

But the transition from white hawthorn to pink thorn (note the progression of colours: the Sonata is white, the Septet will be red) does not give rise to any awakening of the vocation: it is the steeples of Martinville – a work of architecture – that prompt the first attempt, and the trees of Hudimesnil – plants – that issue a summons to the Narrator which he will not understand until later. Here too, however, revelation is possible, as Schopenhauer tells us: 'If, for example, I contemplate a tree aesthetically, i.e., with artistic eyes, and thus recognize not it but its Idea, it is immediately of no importance whether it is this tree or its ancestor that flourished a thousand years ago' (1958, I: 209). In other words, it is not this particular tree that is an object of aesthetic satisfaction but an *essence* of the tree *located outside time*. And it is precisely this that the Narrator does not, at this point, understand:

Had I indeed never seen them before, and did they conceal beneath their surface, like certain trees on tufts of grass that I had seen beside the Guermantes way, a meaning as obscure, as hard to grasp, as is a distant past, so that, whereas they were inviting me to probe a new thought, I imagined that I had to identify an old memory? . . . I chose rather to believe that they were phantoms of the past.   (*WBG*, I: 772–3)

However, there are still some stages to be passed through in order that the revelation may come about. Before arriving at music, we have to proceed via painting. Architecture is at the bottom of the ladder because it is a directly functional art. Painting occupies an intermediate position because it refers to the external world, that is, the world of ideas. It is not surprising, then, that Swann, a critic of painting, should fail, or that the Sonata, in its descriptive phase, should be compared to a painting (it does not matter which one) by Pieter de Hooch (*S*, I: 238). Now, Dutch interiors are cited four times by Schopenhauer (1958, I: 197, 207–8, 210, 230) when he wants to show that painting can provide access to the essence of things from realities of the world which are themselves apparently insignificant.

Yet in *A la recherche*, as in the *World*, it is through music that we can gain access to the superior world of the essence. For Schopenhauer music is indeed, like the other arts, an idea, but because it rises above precise description of the world it is a direct reflection of the Will (1958, I: 257) and of the essence of the Will-to-Live. Elsewhere Schopenhauer anticipates a possible objection:

Perhaps some might take umbrage at the fact that, according to the present metaphysics of music, whereas it so often exalts our minds and seems to speak of worlds different from and better than ours, it nevertheless flatters only the will-to-live, since it depicts the true nature of the will, gives it a glowing account of its success, and at the end expresses its satisfaction and contentment. The following passage from the *Veda* may serve to set at rest such doubts: 'And that rapturous [*sic*] which is a kind of delight is called the highest Atman, because wherever there is a desire, this is part of its delight.' (1958, II: 457)

The philosophy of Schopenhauer is not an apology for suicide (*ibid.*, I: 398–400). Renunciation of the Will-to-Live means that exceptional beings – geniuses and saints – devote themselves to pure contemplation. The musician is the supreme contemplative, for when music does not debase itself in pictorial description (*ibid.*, I: 263–4) it is 'a direct copy of the will itself' (*ibid.*, I: 262).

Is not the joy of the *Veda* also the joyous call to creation that the Narrator hears at the beginning and at the end of the Septet? Yes indeed, it was Schopenhauer who wrote the Vinteuil Sonata (Henry 1981: 8), right down to the last detail: 'The composer reveals the innermost nature of the world, and expresses the profoundest wisdom *in a language that his reasoning faculty does not understand,* just as a magnetic somnambulist gives information about things of which she has no conception when she is awake. Therefore in the composer, more than in any other artist, *the man is entirely separate and distinct from the artist'* (1958, I: 260). Herein reside Swann's false trails: rational explanation, biographical explanation. We should also recall the Narrator's speculation about a phrase in the Septet: 'Perhaps ... it had been inspired in Vinteuil by his daughter's sleep' (*C*, III: 255).

The little phrase that follows the course of Swann's feelings, yet expresses them in a general and therefore changing way, through specific musical data – all this we find again in our philosopher: '[Music] portrays every agitation, every effort, every movement of the will, everything which the faculty of reason summarizes under the wide and negative concept of feeling, and which cannot be further taken up into the abstraction of reason' (1958, I: 259). Further: 'Music does not express this or that particular and definite pleasure, this or that affliction, pain, sorrow, horror, gaiety, merriment, or peace of mind, but joy, pain, sorrow, horror, gaiety, merriment, or peace of mind *themselves*, to a certain extent in the abstract' (*ibid.*, I: 261). But he adds a subtle qualification: 'Its universality is by no means that empty universality of abstraction, but is of quite a different kind; it is united with thorough and unmistakable distinctness' (*ibid.*, I: 262). For Swann, similarly, musical ideas are 'impenetrable to the intellect',* but nonetheless 'perfectly distinct from one another' (*S*, I: 379–80) and even pregnant with religious mystery: 'The inexpressible depth of all music, by virtue of which it floats past us as a paradise quite familiar and yet eternally remote, and is so easy to understand and yet so inexplicable' (1958, I: 264). We are not far from the 'unknown country' (see above, p. 66) that composers of genius reveal to us, even if Anne Henry sees in this the influence of the English aesthetician Pater (1981: 307).

Schopenhauer, in short, assigns to music the same revelatory and transcendent function that it has in Proust, a function which thus defies poietic explanation. It also has the same relationship with time: 'Music is perceived . . . in and through time alone, with absolute exclusion of space, even without the influence of the knowledge of causality, and thus of the understanding. For the tones make the aesthetic impression as effect, and this without our going back to their causes' (1958, I: 266). The Septet just had to be a single, indivisible work, gathering together all the characteristics of the previous ones. Thus it is the perfect embodiment of the Will:

Since it is the one indivisible will, which for this reason is wholly in agreement with itself, and reveals itself in the whole Idea as in an act, its phenomenon, though broken up into a variety of different parts and conditions, must yet again show that unity in a thorough harmony of these. This takes place through a necessary relation and dependence of all the parts on one another, whereby the unity of the Idea is also re-established in the phenomenon.   (1958, I: 157)

In piecing together the manuscript fragments that Vinteuil had left behind at his death, his daughter's friend has brought the Septet out of the 'divided' state to which it would otherwise have been condemned, into the state of 'a single idea' which 'pertains to the world considered as Will'. The redemption that she makes possible is not only

---

*'Human mind' in Scott Moncrieff/Kilmartin. [Trans.]

an existential one (sexuality) or an aesthetic one (the work revealed),
but also a metaphysical one.

Music is particularly well suited to playing this role because it
transcends the representations of inferior orders in the objectivity of
the Will:

all the events that . . . are included by the reasoning faculty in the wide,
negative concept of feeling, can be expressed by the infinite number of possible
melodies, but always in the universality of *mere form without the material*.
(1958, I: 262)

Did not Proust speak of impressions *sine materia*? And, passing
through what we think we may identify as music of Beethoven, it is
the purely dynamic play of musical phrases in the last movement of the
Septet that interests *him*. Besides, this is precisely what Schopenhauer
writes about Beethoven:

But at the same time, all the human passions and emotions speak from this
symphony;[4] joy, grief, love, hatred, terror, hope, and so on in innumerable
shades, yet all, as it were, only in the abstract and without any particularization;
it is their *mere form without the material*, like a mere spirit world *without
matter*.   (1958, II: 450)

Similarly it is the evolution of the Septet from the natural world to
pure form, from descriptive music to profound, 'essential' music, that
we find here:

We certainly have an inclination to realize it [music] while we listen, to clothe it
in the imagination with flesh and bone, and to see in it all the different scenes of
life and nature. On the whole, however, this does not promote an understanding
or enjoyment of it, but rather gives it a strange and arbitrary addition. It is
therefore better to interpret it purely and in its immediacy.   (*Ibid.*, II: 450)

What Proust is describing, then, is all the labour that is necessary in
order to extract the essential purity from its shell of phenomena. Consequently it is not important to know whether Proust the man assigned
the same hierarchy to Debussy, Wagner and Beethoven in real life as
that which emerges from an analysis of the 'musical' episodes in *A la
recherche*. After all, we are concerned with a novel based on a
metaphysical aesthetic whose abstract, theoretical content has been
translated into the human attitudes, actions and feelings that are the
substance of a literary work. What matters is that the music of

Debussy, Wagner and Beethoven – whatever their place in the hierarchy of objectification in relation to the Will – should make it possible for anyone who listens to it to perceive the essence. Now, such perception depends less upon the musical work itself than upon the listener. This is proved by the fact that, in *A la recherche*, various specific types of music – impressionism, leitmotif, string quartet – are supposed to come together in one and the same work, the Septet. So what Proust is describing, in the face of musical fact in general, is above all the work of the intellect, which rejects the reasoning faculty in order to arrive at 'a truth the more' (cf. above, p. 36) through an effort of pure contemplation. Besides, this role of the intellect, as it operates throughout Proust's musical journey, coincides perfectly with the conception of it that he elaborates in the theoretical section of *Time Regained* (III; 897–957).[5] It is this same intellect that, in the *World*, enables us to destroy the Will-to-Live, the harmful effects of the Will, in order to attain to pure contemplation of the atemporal Idea. I cannot resist quoting this crucial passage from *The World as Will and Idea*; it is as Proustian in style as it is in spirit:

Raised up by the power of the mind, we relinquish the ordinary way of considering things, and cease to follow under the guidance of the forms of the principle of sufficient reason merely their relations to one another, whose final goal is always the relation to our own will. Thus we no longer consider the where, the when, the why, and the whither in things, but simply and solely the *what*. Further, we do not let abstract thought, the concepts of reason, take possession of our consciousness, but, instead of all this, devote the whole power of our mind to perception, sink ourselves completely therein, and let our whole consciousness be filled by the calm contemplation of the natural object actually present, whether it be a landscape, a tree, a rock, a crag, a building, or anything else. We *lose* ourselves entirely in this object, to use a pregnant expression; in other words, we forget our individuality, our will, and continue to exist only as pure subject, as clear mirror of the object, so that it is as though the object alone existed without anyone to perceive it, and thus we are no longer able to separate the perceiver from the perception, but the two have become one, since the entire consciousness is filled and occupied by a single image of perception. If, therefore, the object has to such an extent passed out of all relation to something outside it, and the subject has passed out of all relation to the will, what is thus known is no longer the individual thing as such, but the *Idea*, the eternal form, the immediate objectivity of the will at this level. Thus at the same time, the person who is involved in this perception is no longer an individual, for in such perception the individual has lost himself; he is *pure* will-less, painless, timeless *subject of knowledge*.

(1958, I: 178–9; Schopenhauer's emphases)

For Schopenhauer, then, music is the ideal model for what philosophy should have been:

Supposing we succeeded in giving a perfectly accurate and complete explanation of music which goes into detail, and thus a detailed repetition in concepts of what it expresses, this would also be at once a sufficient repetition and explanation of the world in concepts, or one wholly corresponding thereto, and hence the true philosophy.   (1958, I: 264)

This is the same idea that we find in Proust, where music is treated as the ideal and Utopian model for literature (see above, p. 63).

Thus Schopenhauer's great work supplies Proust with the narrative framework for the function of music in his novel. This function is by no means the mere literary conjuring trick, the supreme but artificial feat of skill on the novelist's part, that certain critics seem to think. For Marcel Proust, in fact, as for the symbolists – Mallarmé and Verlaine – it was necessary to 'take back from music its own property'; but this went further for the author of *A la recherche*. Thanks to Schopenhauer, the 'property' of music was not only a particular semiological power: it was also a metaphysical truth. Proust's recourse to music is anything but anecdotal in spirit. It is, in every sense of the word, essential.

5

In conclusion: Quest for the essence and denial of the origin

In trying to show what the Sonata and Septet of Vinteuil owe to Schopenhauer, I have obviously gone against Proust's intentions. If *A la recherche* itself is to be a redemptive work in the image of *Parsifal* or the Septet, it needs to escape from Time and become a pure object of philosophical, literary and aesthetic contemplation; the novel must free itself from its epoch and its author. It was not for nothing that Proust asked Céleste to burn his rough drafts, and there can be no doubt he would have done the same with all his notebooks and jotters if only he had time to experience the feeling that his work was finally complete. In all creative artists obsessed with the absolute – and I shall develop this idea elsewhere – we find the same Utopian effort to efface the poietic dimension. It is Utopian, in the first place, because, as Proust shows very clearly with respect to Wagner, even of itself the text of a writer or composer will always bear traces – whether he likes it or not, and to a greater or lesser degree – of the labour that brought it into existence. It is Utopian, secondly, because the creative artist cannot obliterate all traces of his activity. If he destroys his rough drafts and sketches, his contemporaries will describe them. Even if he kills his contemporaries, that will not prevent the critic from comparing his texts and establishing connections (as I have done in this book). And it is Utopian, in the final analysis, because, while all the metaphysicians in the world may say what they like about the Essence or the Idea being located outside time, the books that deal with it or the works that are supposed to apprehend or translate it will always have been created by a human being, in a given period, in a specific context.

Proust wanted a comprehension of the text to come from the text itself. It was no doubt for this reason that, even as he was breaking lances against external sources of interpretation, he took care to sprinkle his text with 'keys' of a more or less obvious nature. A work of initiation is obliged to be a little esoteric. So he alludes to Beethoven and Debussy, but in a discreet manner. As for the philosopher of Frankfurt, perhaps we should have responded sooner to Mme de Cambremer's injunction in *Time Regained*: 'You must re-read what Schopenhauer says about music' (III: 1041).

We cannot fail to observe that this particular key is provided by Mme de Cambremer, an excellent musician, to be sure, but one whom Proust never misses a chance to mock for her snobbery. Indeed, the Duchess of Guermantes makes fun of her openly: '*Re-read* is pretty rich, I must say. Who does she think she's fooling?' (*ibid.*). David Mendelson has pointed out that, by means of this strategy, Proust gives us his source while at the same time tempering it in an ironic context. He exorcises it, as we might say, to the second degree. I would even venture the hypothesis that Proust, feeling it necessary that his conception of music should be understood within the framework of Schopenhauer's metaphysical system, inserts the source *into the text* so that we no longer need to go outside it.

Certainly there is something disappointing about the presence of Schopenhauer behind Proust's text. But what the writer loses in originality he gains in humanity: nothing is created out of nothing, and every thought comes from somewhere. Once we have got over the initial surprise, however – disagreeable as it may be for certain readers – it gives Proust a new originality. For the Schopenhauerian backdrop to his aesthetics allows us to see how he has brought off the *tour de force* of transforming a philosophical idea into a literary subject from which the original, abstract vocabulary has practically disappeared. In short, the novel has acquired a new dimension together with a new meaning. The meaning of a work, let me repeat, is not only the one we construct when we read the text, from our knowledge, emotions and experience of the world. It is also the meaning it had for the author when he wrote it – one which we may try to reconstruct, even though it is not directly accessible to us.

Proust's critical doctrine – the denial of biographical explanations and connections – has thus been interpreted as anticipating the New

Criticism. We may still, with hindsight, turn him into a precursor of the return to the text, but we must acknowledge the meaning his attitude assumes in the context of Schopenhauerian metaphysics. Both Proust and the philosopher reject etiology because the search for causes diverts us from the one undertaking that, in their eyes, deserves our energies: the quest for the essence. This aim is quite different from the spirit of the Russian formalists or of structuralism.

With these last, to be sure, the search for connections – those connections again! – tends to demonstrate what these theoretical currents of the twentieth century owe to symbolism or to phenomenology. As a result they have rediscovered a certain world of things-in-themselves: atemporal structure, universals, the *Ur-code*! And what is *literaturnost* – literarity – if not the essence of literature? Yet there is an abyss of difference between the quest for essences in Proust and Schopenhauer and the need for an absolute that can be discerned in the structuralists and their predecessors. For in the former there is a rejection of rational explanation and of science: see the remarks of Proust concerning literary criticism and musicologists quoted above (pp. 44–5). In the latter, on the other hand, the structuralist 'essence' constitutes a foundation and justification for *analysis*; analysis here is an attempt to grasp the essence.

The problem is different today. I shall avoid the condescending wink at post-modernism – as if the real future lay behind us – but I must emphasise that we have definitely entered the post-structuralist era. This implies several things. It is no longer possible to believe that meanings reside exclusively 'in' a text. As readers we construct meanings; similarly, the writer has invested them in his discourse; but they are not necessarily the same. Consequently we can no longer give an account of a text solely in terms of its own organisation.[1] At the same time we need to retain the best of what we have gained through structuralism: the creative processes have indeed resulted in an *object*, and this object is indeed what we read.

It is the consequences of this situation that I have tried to put into practice. I have caused the poietic information and the analysis of the text itself to interact. In chapter 2, indeed, the underlying presence of the 'Good Friday Spell' enabled me to clarify the redemptive function of the Septet and the respective place of the real works of Wagner and the imaginary works of Vinteuil in the structure of *A la recherche*. Next, in chapter 3, I addressed myself to the immanent study of the passages in the novel that are devoted to music: seriation of these passages and their paradigmatic superimposition revealed a basic tripartite progression, characteristic both of Proust's musical aesthetics and of his musical perception. This was the stage of description. It already contained elements of explanation, since certain aspects of these passages were clarified in the light of the rest of the novel and since two new composers, Debussy and Beethoven, now added themselves to the spectrum of musical references. But it was only in chapter 4 that the recourse to Schopenhauer enabled us to understand whence the remarkable coherence of Proust's 'system' derives.

Obviously I could have restricted myself to an immanent analysis of the text. But an essential dimension of meaning would have been suppressed, for it is the combination of what may appropriately be called the analysis of the neutral level of the text with the poietic illumination of the text that gives the analysis its depth. In short, I do not believe that the literary or musical essence resides in the text itself, outside time, outside history. By eliminating the poietic dimension we can indeed attempt to grasp the essence, but this is a *magical* attempt, which is itself set in a certain moment in the history of European thought. If there is an essence – though I would prefer the less ontological term 'nature' – it is more likely to be found in the difficult and unstable interaction between the level of poietics, the level of the text and the operations whereby they are perceived.[2]

My reflection on the literary, musical and metaphysical journey which causes Proust to place the quest for the essence at the top of his hierarchy of values leads me, in fact, to question that hierarchy.

For if a Beethoven quartet may give the impression of touching on the ultimate and profound nature of things – a feeling which should no doubt be explained by psychology rather than metaphysics – and even if such a Beethoven quartet must be recognised by everyone as the embodiment of the sublime, nothing prevents us from also observing that it was written at the beginning of the nineteenth century by a certain Beethoven who abandoned it, through the medium of a score, to the uncertain vessel of posterity and to the uncontrollable reactions of his listeners. The work of genius – if there is such a thing as genius – is not an embodiment of the Idea or an image of the Will. It is a contingent representation.

Appendix

PASSAGES FROM *A LA RECHERCHE* TRANSLATED
IN THE TEXT

As this book goes to press, only two volumes of the new (four-volume) Pléiade edition (*NE*) have appeared. For the sake of consistency, therefore, references here are to the old, three-volume Pléiade text, ed. Pierre Clarac and André Ferré (Paris: Gallimard, 1954), with cross-references to the new edition added where possible. Quotations have been cross-checked and discrepancies indicated by { }. Italicised passages correspond to those in the main text. The following abbreviations are used:

CG   *Le Côté de Guermantes*
F   *La Fugitive*
JFF *A l'ombre des jeunes filles en fleurs*
P   *La Prisonnière*
S   *Du côté de chez Swann*
SG   *Sodome et Gomorrhe*
TR   *Le Temps retrouvé*

Page Translation

4–5 [*The little phrase*] . . . '[La petite phrase] était encore là comme une bulle irisée qui se soutient. Tel un arc-en-ciel, dont l'éclat faiblit, s'abaisse, puis se relève et, avant {'et avant' in *NE*} de s'éteindre, s'exalte un moment comme il n'avait pas encore fait: aux deux couleurs qu'elle avait jusque-là laissé paraître, elle ajouta d'autres cordes diaprées, toutes celles du prisme, et les fit chanter' (*S*, I: 352; *NE*, I: 346).

12 *Could life* . . . 'La vie pouvait-elle me consoler de l'art? y avait-il dans l'art une réalité plus profonde où notre personnalité véritable trouve une

expression que ne lui donnent pas les actions de la vie? Chaque grand artiste semble, en effet, si différent des autres, et nous donne tant cette sen. sation de l'individualité que nous cherchons en vain dans l'existence quotidienne! Au moment où je pensais cela, une mesure de la Sonate me frappa, mesure que je connaissais bien pourtant, mais parfois l'attention éclaire différemment des choses connues pourtant depuis longtemps et où nous remarquons ce que nous n'y avions jamais vu. En jouant cette mesure, et bien que Vinteuil fût là en train d'exprimer un rêve qui fût resté tout à fait étranger à Wagner, je ne pus m'empêcher de murmurer: "*Tristan*", avec le sourire qu'a l'ami d'une famille retrouvant quelque chose de l'aïeul dans une intonation, un geste du petit-fils qui ne l'a pas connu. Et comme on regarde alors une photographie qui permet de préciser la ressemblance, par-dessus la Sonate de Vinteuil j'installai sur le pupitre la partition de *Tristan*, dont on donnait justement cet après-midi-là des fragments au concert Lamoureux (*P*, III: 158–9).

13 *I was* . . . 'Je me rendais compte de tout ce qu'a de réel l'oeuvre de Wagner, en revoyant ces thèmes insistants et fugaces qui visitent un acte, ne s'éloignent que pour revenir, et, parfois lointains, assoupis, presque détachés, sont, à d'autres moments, tout en restant vagues, si pressants et si proches, si internes, si organiques, si viscéraux qu'on dirait la reprise moins d'un motif que d'une névralgie' (*ibid.*: 159).

13 *combine* . . . 'réunir diverses individualités' (*ibid.*).

13 *Even that* . . . 'ce qui en elle [la musique] est le plus indépendant du sentiment qu'elle nous fait éprouver, garde sa réalité extérieure et entièrement définie; le chant d'un oiseau, la sonnerie de cor d'un chasseur, l'air que joue un pâtre sur son chalumeau, découpent à l'horizon leur silhouette sonore' (*ibid.*: 160).

15 *The other* . . . 'L'autre musicien, celui qui me ravissait en ce moment, Wagner, tirant de ses tiroirs un morceau délicieux pour le faire entrer comme thème rétrospectivement nécessaire dans une oeuvre à laquelle il ne songeait pas au moment où il l'avait composé, puis ayant composé un premier opéra mythologique, puis un second, puis d'autres encore, et s'apercevant tout à coup qu'il venait de faire une Tétralogie, dut éprouver un peu de la même ivresse que Balzac quand celui-ci . . . s'avisa brusquement . . . qu'ils [ses ouvrages] seraient plus beaux réunis en un cycle où les mêmes personnages reviendraient . . .' (*ibid.*: 160–1).

15 *Vulcan-like* . . . 'habileté vulcanienne' (*ibid.*: 161).

15 *when he* . . . 'quand il découvrit dans sa mémoire l'air du pâtre, l'agrégea à son oeuvre, lui donna toute sa signification' (*ibid.*: 161).

15 *Before the* . . . 'Avant le grand mouvement d'orchestre qui précède le retour d'Yseult, c'est l'oeuvre elle-même qui a attiré à soi l'air de chalumeau à demi oublié d'un pâtre' (*ibid.*: 161).

18 *It was* . . . 'Il me suffisait . . . [que] les boules de neige . . . me rappelassent que l'Enchantement du Vendredi Saint figure un miracle naturel auquel on pourrait assister tous les ans si l'on était plus sage' (*JFF*, I: 635; *NE*, I: 624).

18 *He soon* . . . 'il retrouva bientôt l'expression de béatitude qui lui est habituelle en entendant l'Enchantement du Vendredi-Saint' (*SG*, II: 1105).

31 *I should* . . . 'j'eusse été moins troublé dans un antre magique que dans ce petit salon d'attente où le feu me semblait procéder à des transmutations, comme dans le laboratoire de Klingsor' (*JFF*, I: 527; *NE*, I: 518).

32 *had for me* . . . 'Ce nom, devenu pour moi presque mythologique' (*S*, I: 144; *NE*, I: 142).

35 *The hotel* . . . 'cet hôtel est assez adapté à votre hyperesthésie auditive' (*CG*, II: 72; *NE*, II: 371).

35 *our hearing* . . . 'l'ouïe, ce sens délicieux' (*P*, III: 116).

35 *There are* . . . 'Il y a dans le violon − si, ne voyant pas l'instrument, on ne peut pas rapporter ce qu'on entend à son image, laquelle modife la sonorité − des accents' (*S*, I: 347; *NE*, I: 341).

35–6 *[Albertine]* . . . '[Albertine] choisissait des morceaux ou tout nouveaux ou qu'elle ne m'avait encore joués qu'une fois ou deux, car, commençant à me connaître, elle savait que je n'aimais proposer à mon attention que ce qui m'était encore obscur, et pouvoir, au cours de ces exécutions successives, rejoindre les unes aux autres, grâce à la lumière croissante, mais hélas! dénaturante et étrangère de mon intelligence, les lignes fragmentaires et interrompues de la construction, d'abord presque ensevelie dans la brume. Elle savait, et je crois comprenait la joie que donnait, les premières fois, à mon esprit, ce travail de modelage d'une nébuleuse encore informe. . . Elle devinait qu'à la troisième ou quatrième exécution, mon intelligence, en ayant atteint, par conséquent mis à la même distance, toutes les parties, et n'ayant plus d'activité à déployer à leur égard, les avait réciproquement étendues et immobilisées sur un plan uniforme. Elle ne passait pas cependant encore à un nouveau morceau, car, sans peut-être bien se rendre compte du travail qui se faisait en moi, elle savait qu'au moment où le travail de mon intelligence était arrivé à dissiper le mystère d'une oeuvre, il était bien rare qu'elle n'eût pas, au cours de sa tâche néfaste, attrapé par compensation telle ou telle réflexion profitable. Et le jour où Albertine disait: "Voilà un rouleau que nous allons donner à Françoise pour qu'elle nous le fasse changer contre un autre", souvent il y avait pour moi sans doute un morceau de musique de moins dans le monde, mais une vérité de plus' (*P*, III: 371–2).

37 *There were* . . . 'Il y avait là d'admirables idées que Swann n'avait pas distinguées à la première audition' (*S*, I: 351; *NE*, I: 345).

37 *But often* . . . 'Mais souvent on n'entend rien, si c'est une musique un peu compliquée qu'on écoute pour la première fois' (*JFF*, I: 529; *NE*, I: 520).

37 *even when* . . . 'même quand j'eus écouté la Sonate d'un bout à l'autre, elle me resta presque tout entière invisible' (*JFF*, I: 530; *NE*, I: 521).

37 *the notes* . . . 'les notes sont évanouies avant que ces sensations soient assez formées en nous pour ne pas être submergées par celles qu'éveillent déjà les notes suivantes ou même simultanées. Et cette impression continuerait à envelopper de sa liquidité et de son "fondu" les motifs qui par instants en émergent, à peine discernables, pour plonger aussitôt et disparaître, connus seulement par le plaisir particulier qu'ils donnent, impossibles à décrire, à se rappeler, à nommer, ineffables – si la mémoire, comme un ouvrier qui travaille à établir des fondations durables au milieu des flots, en fabriquant pour nous des fac-similés de ces phrases fugitives, ne nous permettait de les comparer à celles qui leur succèdent et de les différencier. Ainsi, à peine la sensation délicieuse que Swann avait ressentie était-elle expirée, que sa mémoire lui en avait fourni séance tenante une transcription sommaire et provisoire, mais sur laquelle il avait jeté les yeux tandis que le morceau continuait, si bien que, quand la même impression était tout d'un coup revenue, elle n'était déjà plus insaisissable' (*S*, I: 209; *NE*, I: 206).

38 *he now* . . . 'il [les] percevait maintenant, comme si elles se fussent, dans le vestiaire de sa mémoire, débarrassées du déguisement uniforme de la nouveauté' (*S*, I: 351; *NE*, I: 345).

38 *And yet* . . . 'Et pourtant quand plus tard on m'eut joué deux ou trois fois cette Sonate, je me trouvai la connaître parfaitement . . . Probablement ce qui fait défaut, la première fois, ce n'est pas la compréhension, mais la mémoire. Car la nôtre, relativement à la complexité des impressions auxquelles elle a à faire face pendant que nous écoutons, est infime . . . Ces impressions multiples, la mémoire n'est pas capable de nous en fournir immédiatement le souvenir. Mais celui-ci se forme en elle peu à peu' (*JFF*, I: 529–30; *NE*, I: 520).

38 *The time* . . . 'Ce temps du reste qu'il faut à un individu – comme il me le fallut à moi à l'égard de cette Sonate – pour pénétrer une oeuvre un peu profonde, n'est que le raccourci et comme le symbole des années, des siècles parfois, qui s'écoulent avant que le public puisse aimer un chef. d'oeuvre vraiment nouveau' (*JFF*, I: 531; *NE*, I: 521-2).

38 *It was* . . . 'Ce sont les quatuors de Beethoven (les quatuors XII, XIII, XIV et XV) qui ont mis cinquante ans à faire naître, à grossir le public des quatuors de Beethoven, réalisant ainsi comme tous les chefs-d'oeuvre un progrès sinon dans la valeur des artistes, du moins dans la société des esprits, largement composée aujourd'hui de ce qui était introuvable quand

le chef-d'oeuvre parut, c'est-à-dire d'êtres capables de l'aimer. Ce qu'on appelle la postérité, c'est la postérité de l'oeuvre' (*JFF*, I: 531; *NE*, I: 522).

39 *The Duchess* . . . 'La duchesse doit être alliancée avec tout ça, dit Françoise en reprenant la conversation aux Guermantes de la rue de la Chaise, comme on recommence un morceau à l'andante' (*CG*, II: 22; *NE*, II: 322).

39 *Wasn't it* . . . 'N'est-ce pas que c'était bien beau? L'andante, n'est-ce pas? C'est ce qu'on a jamais écrit de plus touchant' (*P*, III: 279).

39 *we might* . . . 'on prierait Charlie . . . de rejouer pour nous seuls le sublime adagio' (*ibid.*: 287).

39 *At first* . . . 'D'abord, il n'avait goûté que la qualité matérielle des sons sécrétés par les instruments' (*S*, I: 208; *NE*, I: 205).

39–40 *But then* . . . 'à un moment donné, *sans pouvoir nettement distinguer un contour*, . . . il avait cherché à recueillir la phrase ou l'harmonie – il ne savait lui-même – qui passait' (*S*, I: 208–9; *NE*, I: 205).

40 *This time* . . . '*Cette fois il avait distingué nettement une phrase* s'élevant pendant quelques instants au-dessus des ondes sonores' (*S*, I: 209; *NE*, I: 206).

40 *Then it* . . . 'Puis elle disparut. Il souhaita passionnément la revoir une troisième fois. Et elle reparut en effet' (*S*, I: 210; *NE*, I: 207).

40 *The music* . . . 'la musique de Vinteuil étendait, notes par notes, touches par touches, les colorations inconnues, inestimables, d'un univers insoupçonné, fragmenté par les lacunes que laissaient entre elles les auditions de son oeuvre' (*P*, III: 255).

40 *Truth* . . . 'A vrai dire, esthétiquement ce motif de joie ne me plaisait pas . . . Il me semblait que Vinteuil avait manqué là d'inspiration, et en conséquence, je manquai aussi là un peu de force d'attention' (*ibid.*: 250–1).

40 *Since I* . . . 'Pour n'avoir pu aimer qu'en des temps successifs tout ce que m'apportait cette Sonate, je ne la possédai jamais tout entière: elle ressemblait à la vie. Mais, moins décevants que la vie, ces grands chefs-d'oeuvre ne commencent pas par nous donner ce qu'ils ont de meilleur' (*JFF*, I: 530–1; *NE*, I: 521).

40 *even within* . . . 'au sein de chacune de ces oeuvres-là . . . ce sont les parties les moins précieuses qu'on perçoit d'abord. . . il nous reste à aimer telle phrase que son ordre, trop nouveau pour offrir à notre esprit rien que confusion, nous {'confusion nous' in *NE*} avait rendue indiscernable et gardée intacte . . . nous l'aimerons plus longtemps que les autres, parce que nous aurons mis plus longtemps à l'aimer' (*JFF*, I: 530–1; *NE*, I: 521).

41 *I don't* . . . 'je n'ai pas envie à force de pleurer de me fiche un rhume de cerveau avec névralgies faciales, comme la dernière fois' (*S*, I: 206; *NE*, I: 203).

41 *The Master* . . . 'Il est vraiment superbe, le Patron! C'est comme si dans la *Neuvième* il disait: nous n'entendrons que le finale, ou dans *les Maîtres* que l'ouverture' (*ibid.*).

41 *purely* . . . 'impressions . . . *purement* musicales', 'mince', 'résistante', 'dense', 'directrice', 'multiforme', 'indivise', 'plane', 'entrechoquée' (*S*, I: 208–9; *NE*, I: 205–6).

42 *breadth* . . . 'largeur', 'ténuité', 'stabilité', 'caprice' (*S*, I: 209; *NE*, I: 206).

42 *symmetrical* . . . 'groupements symétriques', 'la graphie' (*S*, I: 209; *NE*, I: 206).

42 *secret* . . . 'secrète, bruissante et divisée . . . aérienne et odorante', 'dansante, pastorale, intercalée, épisodique' (*S*, I: 211, 218; *NE*, I: 208, 215).

42 *deep blue* . . . 'mauve', 'irisée' (*S*, I: 208, 352; *NE*, I: 205, 346).

42 *the mass* . . . 's'élever en un clapotement liquide, la masse de la partie de piano' (*S*, I: 208; *NE*, I: 206).

42 *the deep* . . . 'la mauve agitation des flots que charme et bémolise le clair de lune' (*ibid.*).

42 *submersion* . . . 'submergées', 'liquidité', 'émergent', 'plonger', 'au milieu des flots', 'au-dessus des ondes sonores' (*S*, I: 209; *NE*, I: 206).

42 *the fragrance* . . . 'odeurs de roses circulant dans l'air humide du soir' (*ibid.*).

42 *fluidity* . . . 'liquidité . . . fondu', 'brume' (*S*, I: 209, *JFF*, I: 530; *NE*, I: 206, *NE*, I: 521).

42 *impressionism* . . . 'impressionisme', 'recherche de la dissonance', 'emploi *exclusif* de la gamme chinoise' (*JFF*, I: 532; *NE*, I: 522).

43 *At first* . . . 'D'abord, il n'avait goûté que la qualité matérielle des sons sécrétés par les instruments' (*S*, I: 208; *NE*, I: 205).

43 *to give* . . . 'donner un nom à ce qui lui plaisait' (*ibid.*).

43 *impossible* . . . 'les motifs [sont] impossibles à décrire, à se rappeler, à nommer, ineffables' (*S*, I: 209; *NE*, I: 206).

43 *He had before* . . . 'il avait devant lui *cette chose qui n'est plus de la musique pure*, qui est du dessin, de l'architecture, de la pensée, et qui permet de se rappeler la musique' (*ibid.*).

43 *He had* . . . 'Depuis si longtemps il avait renoncé à appliquer sa vie à un but idéal et la bornait à la poursuite de satisfactions quotidiennes' (*S*, I: 210; *NE*, I: 207).

43 *like a* . . . 'comme certains valétudinaires . . . [qui] commencent à envisager la possibilité inespérée de commencer sur le tard une vie toute différente, Swann trouvait en lui, dans le souvenir de la phrase qu'il avait entendue . . . la présence d'une de ces réalités invisibles auxquelles il avait cessé de croire et auxquelles . . . il se sentait de nouveau le désir et presque la force de consacrer sa vie' (*S*, I: 211; *NE*, I: 207–8).

44 *Never having* . . . 'n'étant pas arrivé à savoir de qui était l'oeuvre qu'il avait entendue, il n'avait pu se la procurer et avait fini par l'oublier' (*S*, I: 211; *NE*, I: 208).

44 *But now* . . . 'Mais maintenant il pouvait demander le nom de son inconnue (on lui dit que c'était l'andante de la *Sonate pour piano et violon* de

Vinteuil), il la tenait, il pourrait l'avoir chez lui aussi souvent qu'il voudrait, essayer d'apprendre son langage et son secret (*S*, I: 212; *NE*, I: 209).

44 *He asked* . . . 'il demandait des renseignements sur Vinteuil, sur son oeuvre, sur l'époque de sa vie où il avait composé cette sonate, sur ce qu'avait pu signifier pour lui la petite phrase, c'est cela surtout qu'il aurait voulu savoir' (*ibid.*).

44–5 *the futility* . . . 'la vanité des études où on essaye de deviner de qui parle un auteur. Car une oeuvre, même de confession directe, est pour le moins inter- calée entre plusieurs épisodes de la vie de l'auteur, ceux antérieurs qui l'ont inspirée, ceux postérieurs qui ne lui ressemblent pas moins, les amours suivantes étant calquées sur les précédentes' (*TR*, III: 908).

45 *Though* . . . 'C'est même plus beau que l'orchestre, plus complet . . . on n'avoue pas qu'on ne connaît pas la sonate de Vinteuil, on n'a pas le droit de ne pas la connaître . . . on ne perd pas son temps à couper les cheveux en quatre ici' (*S*, I: 212–13; *NE*, I: 209–10).

45 *It appeared* . . . 'Il leur semblait quand le pianiste jouait la sonate qu'il ac- crochait au hasard sur le piano des notes que ne reliaient pas en effet les formes auxquelles ils étaient habitués' (*S*, I: 213; *NE*, I: 210).

45 *caused* . . . 'produit une grande impression dans une école de tendances très avancées' (*S*, I: 214; *NE*, I: 210).

45 *This remark* . . . 'Swann ne trouva pas cette remarque absurde, mais elle le troubla; car *une oeuvre de musique pure* ne contenant aucun des rapports logi- ques dont l'altération dans le langage dénonce la folie, la folie reconnue dans une sonate lui paraissait quelque chose d'aussi mystérieux que la folie d'une chienne, la folie d'un cheval, qui pourtant s'observent en effet' (*S*, I: 214; *NE*, I: 211).

46 *After* . . . 'après une note haute longuement tenue pendant deux mesures, il vit approcher, s'échappant de sous cette sonorité prolongée et tendue com- me un rideau sonore pour cacher le mystère de son incubation, il reconnut, secrète, bruissante et divisée, la phrase aérienne et odorante qu'il aimait' (*S*, I: 211; *NE*, I: 208).

46 [*The pianist*] . . . '[*Le pianiste*] commençait par la tenue des trémolos de violon que pendant quelques mesures on entend seuls, occupant tout le premier plan, puis tout d'un coup ils semblaient s'écarter et, *comme dans ces tableaux de Pieter de Hooch* {'Hooch,' in *NE*} *qu'approfondit le cadre étroit d'une porte entr'ouverte* {'entrouverte' in *NE*}, tout au loin, d'une couleur autre, dans le velouté d'une lumière interposée, la petite phrase apparaissait, dansante, pastorale, intercalée, épisodique, appartenant à un autre monde' (*S*, I: 218; *NE*, I: 215).

47 *dancing* . . . 'dansante . . . intercalée, épisodique', 'secrète, bruissante, divisée' (*S*, I: 218, 211; *NE*, I: 215, 208).

47 *perfumed* . . . 'odorante', 'certaines odeurs de roses', 'pastorale' (*S*, I: 211, 209, 218; *NE*, I: 208, 206, 215).

47 *belongs* . . . 'appartenant à un autre monde', 'immortel' (*S*, I: 218; *NE*, I: 215).

47 *It rippled* . . . 'Elle passait à plis simples et immortels, distribuant çà et là les dons de sa grâce, avec le même ineffable sourire' (*ibid.*).

47 *thought* . . . 'y croyait distinguer maintenant du désenchantement. Elle semblait connaître la vanité de ce bonheur dont elle montrait la voie' (*ibid.*).

47 *a pledge* . . . 'un gage, un souvenir de son amour' (*ibid.*).

47-8 *He almost* . . . 'il regrettait presque qu'elle eût une signification, une beauté intrinsèque et fixe, étrangère à eux' (*S*, I: 219; *NE*, I: 215).

48 *The little* . . . 'La petite phrase continuait à s'associer pour Swann à l'amour qu'il avait pour Odette' (*S*, I: 236; *NE*, I: 233).

48 *in so far* . . . 'à ce que l'affection d'Odette pouvait avoir d'un peu court et décevant, la petite phrase venait ajouter, amalgamer *son essence mystérieuse*' (*S*, I: 237; *NE*, I: 233).

48 *Odette's qualities* . . . 'les qualités d'Odette ne justifiaient pas qu'il attachât tant de prix aux moments passés auprès d'elle' (*S*, I: 236; *NE*, I: 233).

48 *What matter* . . . 'Qu'importait qu'elle lui dît que l'amour est fragile, le sien était si fort!' (*S*, I: 237; *NE*, I: 234).

48 *The pleasure* . . . 'le plaisir que lui donnait la musique et qui allait bientôt créer chez lui un véritable besoin, ressemblait en effet, à ces moments-là, au plaisir qu'il aurait eu à expérimenter des parfums, à entrer en contact avec un monde pour lequel nous ne sommes pas faits' (*S*, I: 237; *NE*, I: 233).

48 *And since* . . . 'Et comme dans la petite phrase il cherchait cependant un sens où son intelligence ne pouvait descendre, quelle étrange ivresse il avait à *dépouiller son âme la plus intérieure de tous les secours du raisonnement* et à la faire passer seule dans le couloir, dans le filtre obscur du son!' (*S*, I: 237; *NE*, I: 234).

49 *Swann* . . . 'Swann, en son coeur s'adressa à elle [la petite phrase] comme à une confidente de son amour, comme à une amie d'Odette qui devrait bien lui dire de ne pas faire attention à ce Forcheville' (*S*, I: 264; *NE*, I: 260).

49 *Beneath* . . . 'sous l'agitation des trémolos de violon qui la protégeaient de leur venue frémissante à deux octaves de là − et comme dans un pays de montagne, derrière l'immobilité apparente et vertigineuse d'une cascade, on aperçoit, deux cents pieds plus bas, la forme minuscule d'une promeneuse − la petite phrase venait d'apparaître, lointaine, gracieuse, protégée par le long déferlement du rideau transparent, incessant et sonore' (*ibid.*).

50 *He suffered* . . . 'Il souffrait de rester enfermé au milieu de ces gens dont la bêtise et les ridicules le frappaient d'autant plus douloureusement qu'ignorant son amour . . . ils le lui faisaient apparaître sous l'aspect d'un état subjectif qui n'existait que pour lui, dont rien d'extérieur ne lui affirmait la réalité' (*S*, I: 344-5; *NE*, I: 339).

50 *Had it* . . . 'si souvent elle avait été témoin de leurs joies! Il est vrai que souvent aussi elle l'avait averti de leur fragilité. Et même, alors que dans ce temps-là il devinait de la souffrance dans son sourire, dans son intonation limpide et désenchantée, *aujourd'hui* il y trouvait plutôt la grâce d'une résignation presque gaie' (*S*, I: 348; *NE*, I: 342).

50 *that the* . . . 'que le sentiment qu'Odette avait eu pour lui ne renaîtrait jamais, que ses espérances de bonheur ne se réaliseraient plus' (*S*, I: 353; *NE*, I: 347).

51 *light* . . . 'légère, apaisante et murmurée', 'une surface obscure', 'douceur rétractée et frileuse' (*S*, I: 348, 350, 349; *NE*, I: 342, 344, 343).

51 *telling him* . . . 'lui *disant* ce qu'elle avait à lui *dire* et dont il scrutait tous les *mots*, regrettant de les voir s'envoler si vite' (*S*, I: 348; *NE*, I: 342).

51 *Swann* . . . 'Swann tenait les motifs musicaux pour de véritables idées' (*S*, I: 349; *NE*, I: 343).

51 *be resolved* . . . 'se résoudre en raisonnements' (*ibid.*).

51 *Vinteuil's phrase* . . . 'la phrase de Vinteuil avait, comme tel thème de *Tristan* par exemple, qui nous représente aussi une certaine acquisition sentimentale . . . pris quelque chose d'humain qui était assez touchant' (*S*, I: 350; *NE*, I: 344).

51 *veiled* . . . 'voilées de ténèbres', 'impénétrables à l'intelligence' (*S*, I: 349; *NE*, I: 343).

51 *none the less* . . . '[elles] n'en sont pas moins parfaitement distinctes les unes des autres, inégales entre elles de valeur et de signification' (*ibid.*).

51 *He had* . . . 'il s'était rendu compte que c'était au faible écart entre les cinq notes qui la composaient et au rappel constant de deux d'entre elles qu'était due cette impression de douceur rétractée et frileuse' (*ibid.*).

51 *in reality* . . . 'en réalité il savait qu'il *raisonnait* ainsi *non sur la phrase elle-même*, mais {'elle-même mais' in *NE*} sur de simples valeurs, *substituées pour la commodité de son intelligence* à la mystérieuse entité qu'il avait perçue' (*ibid.*).

52 *How beautiful* . . . 'Le beau dialogue que Swann entendit entre le piano et le violon au commencement du dernier morceau! La suppression des mots humains, loin d'y laisser régner la fantaisie, comme on avait pu croire, l'en avait éliminée; jamais le langage parlé ne fut si inflexiblement nécessité, ne connut à ce point la pertinence des questions, l'évidence des réponses' (*S*, I: 351; *NE*, I: 345–6).

53 *[Mme de Cambremer]* . . . '[Mme de Cambremer] avait appris dans sa jeunesse à caresser les phrases, au long col sinueux et démesuré, de Chopin, si libres, si flexibles, si tactiles, qui commencent par chercher et essayer leur place en dehors et bien loin de la direction de leur départ, bien loin du point où on avait pu espérer qu'atteindrait leur attouchement, et qui ne se jouent dans cet écart de fantaisie que pour revenir plus délibérément − d'un retour plus prémédité, avec plus de précision, comme sur un cristal qui résonnerait jusqu'à faire crier − vous frapper au coeur' (*S*, I: 331; *NE*, I: 326).

53–4 *an immeasurable* . . . 'un clavier incommensurable, encore presque tout
entier inconnu' (*S*, I: 349; *NE*, I: 344).

54 *What could* . . . 'qu'avait pu être sa vie? au fond de quelles douleurs avait-il
puisé cette force de dieu, cette puissance illimitée de créer?' (*S*, I: 348;
NE, I: 342).

54 *Swann* . . . 'Swann tenait les motifs musicaux pour de véritables idées,
d'un autre monde, d'un autre ordre, idées voilées de ténèbres, inconnues,
impénétrables à l'intelligence, mais qui n'en sont pas moins parfaitement
distinctes les unes des autres, inégales entre elles de valeur et de signification' (*S*, I: 349; *NE*, I: 343).

54 *It* . . . 'elle appartenait pourtant à un ordre de *créatures surnaturelles* et que
nous n'avons jamais vues, mais que malgré cela nous reconnaissons avec
ravissement quand quelque *explorateur de l'invisible* arrive à en capter une,
à l'amener, du monde *divin* où il a accès, briller quelques instants
au-dessus du nôtre' (*S*, I: 351; *NE*, I: 345).

54 *It was* . . . 'Elle était encore là comme une bulle irisée qui se soutient. Tel
un *arc-de-ciel,* dont l'éclat faiblit, s'abaisse, puis se relève et, avant {'et
avant' in *NE*} de s'éteindre, s'exalte un moment comme il n'avait pas
encore fait: aux *deux couleurs* qu'elle avait jusque-là laissé paraître, elle
ajouta d'autres cordes diaprées, toutes celles du *prisme,* et les fit chanter'
(*S*, I: 352; *NE*, I: 346).

55 *Thinking* . . . 'repensant à cette joie extratemporelle causée, soit par le
bruit de la cuiller, soit par le goût de la madeleine, je me disais: "Était-ce
cela, ce bonheur proposé par la petite phrase de la sonate à Swann qui
s'était trompé en l'assimilant au plaisir de l'amour et n'avait pas su le
trouver dans la création artistique, ce bonheur que m'avait fait pressentir
comme plus supra-terrestre encore que n'avait fait la petite phrase de la
sonate, l'appel rouge et mystérieux de ce septuor que Swann n'avait pu
connaître, étant mort comme tant d'autres avant que la vérité faite pour
eux eût été révélée? D'ailleurs, elle n'eût pu lui servir, car cette phrase
pouvait bien symboliser un appel, mais non créer des forces et faire de
Swann l'écrivain qu'il n'était pas" ' (*TR*, III: 877–8).

55 *sometimes* . . . 'Parfois, avant d'aller s'habiller, Mme Swann se mettait au
piano' (*JFF*, I: 529; *NE*, I: 520).

56 *Even when* . . . 'même grand j'eus écouté la Sonate d'un bout à l'autre, elle
me resta presque tout entière invisible, comme un monument dont la
distance ou la brume ne laissent apercevoir que de faibles parties' (*JFF*, I:
530; *NE*, I: 521).

56 *The moment* . . . 'Le moment où il fait nuit sous les arbres, où les arpèges du
violon font tomber la fraîcheur. Avouez que c'est bien joli; il y a là tout le côté
statique du clair de lune, qui est le *côté essentiel*' (*JFF*, I: 533; *NE*, I: 523).

56 *That's what* . . . 'C'est cela qui est si bien peint dans cette petite phrase,
c'est le Bois de Boulogne tombé en catalepsie . . . je compris par d'autres

propos de lui que ces feuillages nocturnes étaient tout simplement ceux sous l'épaisseur desquels, dans maint restaurant des environs de Paris, il avait entendu, bien des soirs, la petite phrase. Au lieu du sens profond qu'il lui avait si souvent demandé, ce qu'elle rapportait à Swann, c'était ces feuillages rangés, enroulés, peints autour d'elle . . . c'était tout un printemps dont il n'avait pu jouir autrefois' (*JFF*, I: 533; *NE*, I: 523–4).

56 *Vinteuil's phrase* . . . 'la phrase de Vinteuil ne me montre que tout ce à quoi je ne faisais pas attention à cette époque. De mes soucis, de mes amours de ce temps-là, elle ne me rappelle plus rien, elle a fait l'échange' (*JFF*, I: 534; *NE*, I: 524).

56–7 *What the* . . . 'ce que la musique montre – du moins à moi – ce n'est pas du tout la "Volonté en soi" et la "Synthèse de l'infini", mais, par exemple, le père Verdurin en redingote dans le Palmarium du Jardin d'Acclimatation' (*ibid.*).

57 *I did* . . . 'je ne m'attachai pas à remarquer combien la combinaison du motif voluptueux et du motif anxieux répondait davantage maintenant à mon amour pour Albertine' (*P*, III: 158).

57 *Approaching* . . . 'prenant la Sonata à un autre point de vue, la regardant en soi-même comme l'oeuvre d'un grand artiste, j'étais ramené par le flot sonore vers les jours de Combray – je ne veux pas dire de Montjouvain et du côté de Méséglise, mais des promenades du côté de Guermantes – où j'avais moi-même désiré d'être un artiste' (*ibid.*).

58 *that sensation* . . . 'cette sensation de l'individualité que nous cherchons en vain dans l'existence quotidienne' (*ibid.*).

58 *It was* . . . 'elle était si particulière, elle avait un charme si individuel' (*S*, I: 211; *NE*, I: 208).

58 *Music* . . . 'La musique, bien différente en cela de la société d'Albertine, m'aidait à descendre en moi-même, à y découvrir du nouveau: la variété que j'avais en vain cherchée dans la vie, dans le voyage, dont pourtant la nostalgie m'était donnée par ce flot sonore qui faisait mourir à côté de moi ses vagues ensoleillées' (*P*, III: 159).

58 *the song* . . . 'le chant d'un oiseau, la sonnerie de cor d'un chasseur, l'air que joue un pâtre sur son chalumeau' (*ibid.*: 160).

58 *Could it* . . . 'Serait-ce elle qui donnerait chez les grands artistes l'*illusion* d'une originalité foncière, irréductible, en apparence reflet d'une réalité plus qu'humaine, en fait produit d'un *labeur industrieux*? Si l'art n'est que cela, il n'est pas plus réel que la vie, et je n'avais pas tant de regrets à avoir. Je continuais à jouer *Tristan*' (*ibid.*: 161–2).

58 *However* . . . 'si haut qu'on plane, on est un peu empêché de goûter le silence des espaces par le puissant ronflement du moteur!' (*ibid.*: 162).

59 *In the* . . . 'au sein de ce septuor, des éléments différents s'exposaient tour à tour pour se combiner à la fin' (*ibid.*: 252).

59 [*His*] *Sonata* . . . 'sa Sonate, et comme je le sus plus tard, ses autres oeuvres, n'avaient toutes été, par rapport à ce septuor, que de timides essais, délicieux mais bien frêles, auprès du chef-d'oeuvre triomphal et complet qui m'était en ce moment révélé' (*ibid.*).

59 *I could* . . . 'je ne pouvais m'empêcher, par comparaison, de me rappeler que . . . j'avais pensé aux autres mondes qu'avait pu créer Vinteuil comme à des univers clos comme avait été chacun de mes amours; mais, en réalité . . . si je considérais maintenant non plus mon amour pour Albertine, mais toute ma vie, mes autres amours n'y avaient été que de minces et timides essais qui préparaient, des appels qui réclamaient ce plus vaste amour: l'amour pour Albertine' (*ibid.*).

60 *Something* . . . 'quelque chose de plus mystérieux que l'amour d'Albertine semblait promis au début de cette oeuvre, dans ces premiers cris d'aurore' (*ibid.*: 253).

60 *This Vinteuil* . . . 'Ce Vinteuil que j'avais connu si timide et si triste, avait, quand il fallait choisir un timbre, lui en unir un autre, des audaces, et, dans tout le sens du mot, un bonheur sur lequel l'audition d'une oeuvre de lui ne laissait aucun doute' (*ibid.*: 254).

60 *Vinteuil* . . . 'Vinteuil était mort depuis nombre années; mais, au milieu de ces instruments qu'il avait aimés, il lui avait été donné de poursuivre, pour un temps illimité, une part au moins de sa vie. De sa vie d'homme seulement? Si l'art n'était vraiment qu'un prolongement de la vie, valait-il de lui rien sacrifier? N'était-il pas aussi irréel qu'elle-même? A mieux écouter ce septuor, je ne le pouvais pas penser' (*ibid.*: 254-5).

60–1 *For those* . . . 'Ces phrases-là [de Vinteuil], les musicographes pourraient bien trouver leur apparentement, leur généalogie, dans les oeuvres d'autres grands musiciens, mais seulement pour des raisons accessoires, des ressemblances extérieures, des analogies, plutôt ingénieusement trouvées par le raisonnement que senties par l'impression directe. Celle que donnaient ces phrases de Vinteuil était différente de tout autre, comme si, en dépit des conclusions qui semblent se dégager de la science, l'individuel existait' (*ibid.*: 255-6).

61 *Could it* . . . *Serait-ce* [cette habileté vulcanienne] qui donnerait chez les grands artistes l'illusion d'une originalité foncière, irréductible, en apparence reflet d'une réalité plus qu'humaine, en fait produit d'un labeur industrieux?' (*ibid.*: 161-2).

61 *It was* . . . 'c'était justement quand [Vinteuil] cherchait puissamment à être nouveau, qu'on reconnaissait, sous les différences apparentes, les similitudes profondes et les ressemblances voulues qu'il y avait au sein d'une oeuvre' (*ibid.*: 256).

61 *When Vinteuil* . . . 'quand Vinteuil reprenait à diverses reprises une même

phrase, la diversifiait, s'amusait à changer son rythme, à la faire reparaître sous sa forme première, ces ressemblances-là, voulues, oeuvre de l'intelligence, *forcément superficielles*, n'arrivaient jamais à être aussi frappantes que ces ressemblances dissimulées, involontaires, qui éclataient sous des couleurs différentes, entre les deux chefs-d'oeuvre distincts; car alors Vinteuil, cherchant puissamment à être nouveau, s'interrogeait lui-même, de toute la puissance de son effort créateur atteignait sa propre essence à ces profondeurs où, quelque question qu'on lui pose, c'est du même accent, le sien propre, qu'elle répond. Un accent, cet accent de Vinteuil' (*ibid*.).

61 *analytical* . . . 'des formes analytiques du raisonnement' (*ibid*.).

61 *This was* . . . 'c'était une oeuvre inédite de Vinteuil où il s'était seulement amusé . . . à y faire apparaître un instant la petite phrase' (*ibid*.: 249).

62 *prayer* . . . 'prière', 'spéculation . . . dans le monde des anges', 'ronde divine', 'l'espérance mystique de l'Ange écarlate du Matin' (*ibid*.: 255, 256, 260, 263).

62 *The only* . . . 'Le seul véritable voyage, le seul bain de Jouvence, ce ne serait pas d'aller vers de nouveaux paysages, mais d'avoir d'autres yeux, de voir l'univers avec les yeux d'un autre, de cent autres, de voir les cent univers que chacun d'eux voit, que chacun d'eux est; et cela nous le pouvons avec un Elstir, avec un Vinteuil, avec leurs pareils, nous volons vraiment d'étoiles en étoiles' (*ibid*.: 258).

62–3 *We can* . . . 'nous pouvons en mesurer la profondeur, mais pas plus la traduire en langage humain que ne le peuvent les esprits désincarnés quand, évoqués par un médium, celui-ci les interroge sur les secrets de la mort . . . Chaque artiste semble ainsi comme le citoyen d'une patrie inconnue, oubliée de lui-même' (*ibid*.: 256–7).

63 *I wondered* . . . *'je me demandais si la Musique n'était pas l'exemple unique de ce qu'aurait pu être – s'il n'y avait pas eu l'invention du langage, la formation des mots, l'analyse des idées – la communication des âmes. Elle est comme une possibilité qui n'a pas eu de suites; l'humanité s'est engagée dans d'autres voies, celles du langage parlé et écrit'* (*ibid*.: 258).

63 *as things* . . . 'comme reviennent les choses dans la vie' (*ibid*.: 259).

63 *This phrase* . . . 'cette phrase était ce qui aurait pu le mieux caractériser . . . ces impressions qu'à des intervalles éloignés je retrouvais dans ma vie comme les points de repère, les amorces pour la construction *d'une vie véritable*' (*ibid*.: 261).

63 *Real life* . . . 'La vraie vie, la vie enfin découverte et éclaircie, la seule vie par conséquent réellement vécue, c'est la littérature' (*TR*, III: 895).

63 *ineffable joy* . . . 'joie ineffable qui semblait venir du paradis . . . serait-elle jamais réalisable pour moi?' (*P*, III: 260–1).

64 *It was* . . . 'c'était sur des surfaces unies et planes comme celles de la mer

que, par un matin d'orage, commençait, au milieu d'un aigre silence, dans un vide infini, l'oeuvre nouvelle, et c'est dans un rose d'aurore que, pour se construire progressivement devant moi, cet univers inconnu était tiré du silence et de la nuit' (*ibid.*: 250).

64 *a mystical* . . . 'un mystique chant du coq' (*ibid.*).

64 *the ineffable* . . . 'un appel, ineffable mais suraigu, de l'éternel matin' (*ibid.*).

64 *The atmosphere* . . . 'L'atmosphère froide, lavée de pluie, électrique . . . changeait à tout instant, effaçant la promesse empourprée de l'Aurore' (*ibid.*).

64 *At noon* . . . 'A midi pourtant, dans un ensoleillement brûlant et passager, elle [l'atmosphère] semblait s'accomplir en un bonheur lourd, villageois et presque rustique, où la titubation des cloches retentissantes et déchaînées . . . semblait matérialiser la plus épaisse joie' (*ibid.*).

64 *first cries* . . . 'premiers cris d'aurore' (*ibid.*: 253).

64 *the still* . . . 'la rougeur encore inerte du ciel matinal au-dessus de la mer' (*ibid.*: 255).

65 *We could* . . . 'nous discernâmes, à peine séparées du lumineux azur, *sortant des eaux, roses*, argentines, imperceptibles, les *petites cloches* de l'*angelus* qui sonnaient aux environs de Féterne. "Ceci est encore assez *Pelléas*, fis-je remarquer à Mme de Cambremer-Legrandin. Vous savez la scène que je veux dire." ' (*SG*, II: 822).

65 *the sonata* . . . 'la Sonate s'ouvrait sur une aube liliale et champêtre' (*P*, III: 250).

65 *honeysuckles* . . . 'chèvrefeuilles', 'géraniums blancs', 'monde virginal et meublé de végétaux' (*ibid.*).

65 *the questioning* . . . 'les phrases interrogatives s'y faisaient plus pressantes, plus inquiètes, les réponses plus mystérieuses; l'air délavé du matin et du soir semblait y influencer jusqu'aux cordes des instruments' (*ibid.*: 257).

65 *If these* . . . 'si ces êtres [les deux motifs] s'affrontaient, *c'était débarrassés de leur corps physique, de leur apparence, de leur nom*, et trouvant chez moi un spectateur intérieur – insoucieux lui aussi des noms et du particulier – pour s'intéresser à *leur combat immatériel et dynamique* et en suivre avec passion *les péripéties sonores*' (*ibid.*: 260).

66 *Each artist* . . . 'Chaque artiste semble ainsi comme le citoyen d'une patrie inconnue, oubliée de lui-même, différente de celle d'où viendra, appareillant pour la terre, un autre grand artiste. Tout au plus, de cette patrie, Vinteuil dans ses dernières oeuvres semblait s'être rapproché. L'atmosphère n'y était plus la même que dans la Sonate, *les phrases interrogatives s'y faisaient plus pressantes*, plus inquiètes, les réponses plus mystérieuses; l'air délavé du matin et du soir semblait y influencer

jusqu'aux *cordes* des instruments. Morel avait bien jouer merveilleuse-
ment, *les sons que rendait son violon me parurent singulièrement perçants,
presque criards. Cette âcreté* plaisait et, comme dans certaines voix, on y
sentait *une sorte de qualité morale et de supériorité intellectuelle* . . . le public
le plus intelligent ne s'y trompe pas puisque *l'on déclara plus tard les dernières oeuvres de Vinteuil les plus profondes.* Or aucun programme, aucun
sujet n'apportait un élément intellectuel de jugement. On devinait donc
qu'il s'agissait d'*une transposition, dans l'ordre sonore, de la profondeur'*
(*ibid.*: 257).

68 *Thus* . . . 'Telle, toutes les deux minutes, la même question semblait in-
tensément posée à Jupien dans l'oeillade de M. de Charlus, comme ces
phrases interrogatives de Beethoven, répétées indéfiniment, à intervalles
égaux, et destinées – avec un luxe exagéré de préparations – à amener
un nouveau motif, un changement de ton, une "rentrée" ' (*SG*, II: 605).

68–9 *But let* . . . 'qu'on songe plutôt à tant d'écrivains qui, mécontents du
morceau qu'ils viennent d'écrire, s'ils lisent un éloge du génie de
Chateaubriand ou évoquent tel grand artiste dont ils ont souhaité d'être
l'égal, fredonnant par exemple en eux-mêmes *telle phrase de Beethoven* de
laquelle ils comparent la tristesse à *celle qu'ils ont voulu mettre dans leur
prose*, se remplissent tellement de cette idée de génie qu'ils l'ajoutent à
leurs propres productions en repensant à elles, ne les voient plus telles
qu'elles leur étaient apparues d'abord, et risquant un acte de foi dans la
valeur de leur oeuvre se disent: "Après tout!" sans se rendre compte que,
dans le total qui détermine leur satisfaction finale, ils font entrer le
souvenir de merveilleuses pages de Chateaubriand qu'ils assimilent aux
leurs, mais enfin qu'ils n'ont point écrites' (*JFF*, I: 481; *NE*, I: 472).

69 [*Mlle Vinteuil's friend*] . . . 'l'amie de Mlle Vinteuil eut la consolation
d'assurer au musicien dont elle avait assombri les dernières années une
gloire immortelle et compensatrice' (*P*, III: 262).

70 *It was* . . . 'c'était grâce à elle . . . qu'avait pu venir jusqu'à moi l'étrange
appel que je ne cesserais plus jamais d'entendre comme la promesse qu'il
existait autre chose, réalisable par l'art sans doute, que le néant que j'avais
trouvé dans tous les plaisirs et dans l'amour même, et que si ma vie me
semblait si vaine, du moins n'avait-elle pas tout accompli' (*ibid.*: 263).

70 *Compared* . . . 'A côté de ce Septuor, certaines phrases de la Sonate, que
seules le public connaissait, apparaissaient comme tellement banales qu'on
ne pouvait pas comprendre comment elles avaient pu exciter tant d'admiration' (*ibid.*: 263).

72 *It seemed* . . . 'il me semblait que j'étais moi-même ce dont parlait
l'ouvrage: une église, un *quatuor*, la rivalité de François Ier et de Charles-
Quint' (*S*, I: 3; *NE*, I: 3).

73 *This music* . . . 'cette musique me semblait *quelque chose de plus vrai que tous les livres connus*. Par instants je pensais que cela tenait à ce que ce qui est senti par nous de la vie, ne l'étant pas sous forme d'idées, sa traduction littéraire, c'est-à-dire intellectuelle, en rend compte, l'explique, l'analyse, mais ne le recompose pas comme la musique où les sons semblent prendre l'inflexion de l'être, reproduire cette pointe intérieure et extrême des sensations qui est la partie que nous donne cette ivresse spécifique que nous retrouvons de temps en temps' (*P*, III: 374).

74 *Perhaps* . . . 'Cette qualité inconnue d'un monde unique et qu'aucun musicien ne nous avait jamais fait voir, peut-être était-ce en cela, disais-je à Albertine, qu'est la preuve la plus authentique du génie, bien plus que le contenu de l'oeuvre elle-même. "Même en littérature? me demandait Albertine. − Même en littérature." Et, repensant à la monotonie des oeuvres de Vinteuil, j'expliquais à Albertine que les grands littérateurs n'ont jamais fait qu'une seule oeuvre, ou plutôt réfracté à travers des milieux divers une même beauté qu'ils apportent au monde. "S'il n'était pas si tard, ma petite, lui disais-je, je vous montrerais cela chez tous les écrivains que vous lisez pendant que je dors, je vous montrerais la même identité que chez Vinteuil" ' (*ibid.*: 375).

74 *I began* . . . 'Je me remettais à douter, je me disais qu'après tout il se pourrait que si les phrases de Vinteuil semblaient l'expression de certains états de l'âme analogues à celui que j'avais éprouvé en goûtant la madeleine trempée dans la tasse de thé, rien ne m'assurait que le vague de tels états fût une marque de leur profondeur, mais seulement de ce que nous n'avons pas encore su les analyser, qu'il n'y aurait donc rien de plus réel en eux que dans d'autres' (*ibid.*: 381).

76 *in the* . . . 'dans le seul milieu où [l'être peut] vivre, jouir de l'essence des choses, c'est-à-dire en dehors du temps' (*TR*, III: 871).

76 *Our vanity* . . . 'Ce travail qu'avaient fait notre amour-propre, notre passion, notre esprit d'imitation, notre intelligence abstraite, nos habitudes, c'est ce travail que l'art défera, *c'est la marche en sens contraire, le retour aux profondeurs* où ce qui a existé réellement gît inconnu de nous, qu'il nous fera suivre' (*ibid.*: 896).

77 *Because* . . . 'Parce qu'elle se croyait "avancée" et (en art seulement) "jamais assez à gauche", elle se représentait non seulement que la musique progresse, mais sur une seule ligne, et que Debussy était en quelque sorte un sur-Wagner, encore un peu plus avancé que Wagner' (*SG*, II: 815).

77 *She did* . . . 'Elle ne se rendait pas compte que, si Debussy n'était pas aussi indépendant de Wagner qu'elle-même devait le croire dans quelques années, parce qu'on se sert tout de même des armes conquises pour achever de s'affranchir de celui qu'on a momentanément vaincu, il cherchait

cependant, après la satiété qu'on commençait à avoir des oeuvres trop
complètes, où tout est exprimé, à contenter un besoin contraire' (*ibid.*).

81 *They went* . . . 'elles m'offraient indéfiniment le même charme avec une
profusion inépuisable, mais sans me laisser approfondir davantage, comme
ces mélodies qu'on rejoue cent fois de suite sans descendre plus avant dans
leur secret' (*S*, I: 138; *NE*, I: 136).

82 *Had I* . . . 'ne les avais-je jamais vus et cachaient-ils derrière eux, comme
{'eux comme' in *NE*} tels arbres, telle touffe d'herbe que j'avais vus du
côté de Guermantes, un sens aussi obscur, aussi difficile à saisir qu'un
passé lointain, de {'lointain de' in *NE*} sorte que, sollicité par eux d'approfondir une pensée, je croyais avoir à reconnaître un souvenir? . . . Je
crus plutôt que c'étaient des fantômes du passé' (*JFF*, I: 719; *NE*, I: 78).

83 *Perhaps* . . . 'avait-elle été inspirée à Vinteuil par le sommeil de sa fille [?]'
(*P*, III: 253).

89 *You must* . . . 'Relisez ce que Schopenhauer dit de la musique' (*TR*, III:
992).

89 *Re-read* . . . '*Relisez* est un chef-d'oeuvre! Ah! non, çà, par exemple, il ne
faut pas nous la faire' (*ibid.*).

112 *a change* . . . 'un changement de décor comparable à celui qui introduit
tout à coup Parsifal au milieu des filles-fleurs' (*CG*, II: 423; *NE*, II: 716).

114 *Only* . . . 'Seule l'impression . . . est un critérium de vérité, et à cause de
cela mérite seule d'être appréhendée par l'esprit, car elle est seule capable,
s'il sait en dégager cette vérité, de l'amener à une plus grande perfection
et de lui donner une pure joie. L'impression est pour l'écrivain ce qu'est
l'expérimentation pour le savant, avec cette différence que chez le savant
le travail de l'intelligence précède et chez l'écrivain vient après' (*TR*, III:
880).

FURTHER REFERENCES

Page	Scott Moncrieff/Kilmartin	Pléiade
8	*S*, I: 224–34	*S*, I: 206–14; *NE*, I: 203–11
8	*S*, I: 238–9	*S*, I: 218–19; *NE*, I: 214–16
8	*S*, I: 258–60	*S*, I: 236–8; *NE*, I: 232–4
8	*S*, I: 288	*S*, I: 264; *NE*, I: 260
8	*S*, I: 295	*S*, I: 270–1; *NE*, I: 266
8	*S*, I: 375–84	*S*, I: 344–53; *NE*, I: 339–47
8	*WBG*, I: 570–5	*JFF*, I: 529–34; *NE*, I: 520–5
8	*C*, III: 154–9	*P*, III: 158–62
8	*C*, III: 250–65	*P*, III: 248–64

8	*C*, III: 378–90	*P*, III: 371–84
37	*S*, I: 227	*S*, I: 208; *NE*, I: 205
41	*S*, I: 224–34	*S*, I: 206–14; *NE*, I: 203–11
42	*WBG*, I: 573	*JFF*, I: 532; *NE*, I: 522
46	*S*, I: 238–9	*S*, I: 218–19; *NE*, I: 214–16
48	*S*, I: 258–60	*S*, I: 236–8; *NE*, I: 232–4
49	*S*, I: 288	*S*, I: 264; *NE*, I: 260
49	*S*, I: 295	*S*, I: 270–1; *NE*, I: 266
49	*S*, I: 230	*S*, I: 211; *NE*, I: 208
49	*S*, I: 238	*S*, I: 218; *NE*, I: 214–16
49	*S*, I: 227	*S*, I: 208; *NE*, I: 206
50	*S*, I: 313	*S*, I: 287; *NE*, I: 282
50	*S*, I: 310, 313	*S*, I: 284, 287; *NE*, I: 279, 282
50	*S*, I: 375–84	*S*, I: 344–53; *NE*, I: 339–47
52	*S*, I: 357	*S*, I: 328; *NE*, I: 322
52	*S*, I: 238	*S*, I: 218; *NE*, I: 215
53	*S*, I: 357	*S*, I: 327; *NE*, I: 322
53	*S*, I: 357	*S*, I: 328; *NE*, I: 322
53	*S*, I: 361	*S*, I: 331; *NE*, I: 326
55	*WBG*, I: 570–5	*JFF*, I: 529–34; *NE*, I: 520–5
57	*C*, III: 154–9	*P*, III: 158–62
58	*S*, I: 381	*S*, I: 350; *NE*, I: 344
59	*C*, III: 250–65	*P*, III: 248–64
66	*WBG*, I: 564	*JFF*, I: 531; *NE*, I: 522
69	*S*, I: 196–8	*S*, I: 180; *NE*, I: 178
69	*S*, I: 173–80	*S*, I: 159ff.; *NE*, I: 157ff.
73	*C*, III: 378–90	*P*, III: 371–84
82	*S*, I: 238	*S*, I: 218; *NE*, I: 215

Notes

1 Introduction: Beyond the 'little phrase'

1 Such as the frequently cited allusion to *La Mer* at the beginning of the Septet, where Debussy's name is not mentioned.

2 The subject of a Master's dissertation at the Sorbonne (Pesson 1980). Cf. the review by Danièle Laster (1981).

3 There are numerous studies of Proust's interest in this and that composer. In my opinion, these do more to complete our knowledge of Proust the man than they contribute to the meaning of *A la recherche*. See, for example, Guichard (1963: 220–32), Coeuroy (1923), Mein (1971), Persiani (1970), de Souza (1969), Schneider (1971).

4 On this point, cf. a remark made by Henri Bonnet in his review (1976: 347) of Milly's book.

5 Cf. another version of the Sonata given in Abatangel 1937: 25–46, and a first version of the passage concerning the Septet in Milly 1975: 147. The Pléiade editions reproduce the draft of a description of a quintet and organ concert at Balbec (first Pléiade edition I: 978–82; *NE*, II: 1013–16; [Scott Moncrieff/Kilmartin I: 1028–32]). In the new Pléiade edition (vol. I) the earliest descriptions of the Sonata, which is attributed to Saint-Saëns, are retained in the 1910 drafts of 'Swann in love' (Esquisses LXXIV and LXXV in *NE*, I: 898–950).

6 Cf. the study of the 'danger of metaphor' in Piette 1985: 91–101.

7 Following a convention adopted in most studies of Proust, I refer to his works by abbreviations. These are explained in the Translator's note (see above, pp. xiii–xiv).

8 Jean-Yves Tadié has drawn attention to a forgotten article by Proust which appeared in the *Revue blanche* of April 1893:

> Poor [Franck] is dead, loved . . . by a small number of faithful disciples to whom the ten authentic masterpieces of his mind and heart

had revealed a new world of supreme impressions and inexpressible emotions. The day we learnt of the death of this noble artist, who was so curiously underestimated, we could see that very few appreciated the loss just suffered by Art. People, even the cultured, even those who keep up to date with musical developments, were asking with an air of surprise who Franck was and what he had written. Some of them *knew* him, however: he was a teacher, who hid himself away over the left bank, far away, oh, so very far away; he was conscientious, too, and charged much less for his lessons, when all was said and done, than Marmontel . . . (quoted in Tadié 1983: 36–7)

Here we find observations strikingly similar to the portrait of Vinteuil as an old man.

9 Besides, there are too few technical details in his descriptions of the Sonata or the Septet for a specific model to be recognisable.

10 A complete list is found in Matoré and Mecz (1972).

11 Unless otherwise indicated all emphases within quoted material are mine.

2 *Parsifal as redemptive model for the redemptive work*

1 Tadié (1983: 29) gives as a source for this sentence a letter from Wagner to Liszt of 20 November 1851, which was published in French in 1900. In this letter Wagner explains how he had the idea of prefacing *Siegfrieds Tod* (the original title for *Götterdämmerung*) with *Der junge Siegfried* (which became *Siegfried*) and how he then felt obliged to 'present my myth in its entirety and in all its profundity of meaning' by adding what would later become *Das Rheingold* and *Die Walküre* (Wagner and Liszt 1943: 131–3). But as I shall show below, Proust's formulation is too extreme in relation to the actual genesis of *The Ring*.

2 Boulez has commented on this Proustian comprehension of Wagner's poietics in the following terms:

This description suggests that Proust completely understood how Wagner worked, never going back on himself but always using the same motifs, the same basic resources, in order to achieve a continuous development that is both extremely concise and extremely free. This passage in Proust on the third act of *Tristan* is one of the most impressive things ever written about Wagner. (1976: 52–3)

3 As Deathridge (1984: 41) has pointed out, Wagner himself invalidated this statement by telling Cosima that he had made up the story himself (*Cosima Wagner's Diaries*, 22 April 1879).

4 See Newman 1933: 159–61, 1949: 38–54; von Westernhagen 1962: 38–54, 1963: 178–82, 1976: 17–20. For a 'composite' transcription of the relevant

sketches, see Bailey 1968: 459–94. A complete transcription is due to appear in Werner Breig's dissertation 'Studien zur Entstehungsgeschichte von Wagners *Ring des Nibelungen*'.

5 See *Wagner androgyne* (in preparation).

6 This point will be explained in *Wagner androgyne*.

7 Unless otherwise indicated all emphases within quoted material are mine.

8 It is clear that Proust had this rough draft in mind when he described the reappearance of the little phrase in the last movement of the Sonata (I: 351–2; *NE*, I: 346; [Scott Moncrieff/Kilmartin I: 381–3]). I am grateful to Derrick Puffett for drawing this to my attention.

9 I shall return to this point when considering the various stages of the quest in chapter 3 (see below, p. 58).

10 Another significant allusion: in *The Guermantes Way*, Proust evokes 'a change of surroundings comparable to that which introduces Parsifal suddenly into the midst of the flower-maidens' (*G*, II: 439).

11 Is the name Guermantes a French form of Gurnemanz? My comparison, together with the crucial role played by names in *A la recherche*, permits me to put forward at least the hypothesis.

3 Music as redemptive model for literature

1 This analysis is supported by the recent publication of certain rough drafts for *A la recherche* in the new Pléiade edition. Cf. the following sketch of 1910–11, written at a time when the little phrase is no longer merely a catalyst for involuntary memory, as in *Jean Santeuil*, but leads from dim perception to transcendent revelation:

> For a musical phrase, more than anything else in the world – one might almost wonder if it is not the only thing, apart from love – suggests a kind of desire, of happiness, of voluptuous pleasure which is peculiar to it, which it indicates to us in a mysterious fashion (though clearly enough for us to be aware of it) and which can only be satisfied by it. While it develops, our pleasure focuses and the path that it shows us becomes clear. *The second and third steps* mysteriously summoned up by the initial fervour are enough to promise us the noblest and calmest types of happiness (although these superlatives and these generalisations cannot adequately describe something that is as particular to a phrase as the charm of a new woman whom we love is particular to that woman). Thus the invisible stranger leads us into darkness. But *at the third step*, at the moment when we think it is about to recede, a light bound carries it gaily towards us, and this immediately opens up to us an unexpected path which intensifies our pleasure and leads us into a new world like a child who would eat an apple but, perceiving

that it is eating it between a woman's breasts, sees its calmly gluttonous pleasure turning into a more oblique and enervating type of pleasure. However, sexual pleasure, gluttony, drunkenness and perfumes provide fixed pleasures which are always the same. The world that each beautiful phrase of music opens up to us belongs to it and to it alone.

(*NE*, I: 1239; my emphases)

2 I leave aside the question of whether these characteristics, such as can be inferred from an analysis of the novel, are peculiar to Proust or whether they relate to universal constants of musical perception – indeed of human perception in general. I am inclined to think that these constants are universal, but in order to make a definite assertion one would have to study similar evidence in other writers and compare it with experimental research currently being carried out in this area.

3 Unless otherwise indicated all emphases within quoted material are mine.

4 Note that this perceptive description of Chopin's style is given to Mme de Cambremer, to whom, as I shall show below (p. 89), Proust entrusts his most profound thoughts on music.

5 These two sentences closely echo, in the interrogative, the formulation in the preceding passage: 'If art is no more than that, it is no more real than life' (*C*, III: 159).

6 There is indeed a 'tender' and 'heavenly' phrase (*C*, III: 260) in the Andante of the Septet, but it is not identified as the little phrase, merely compared to it (*ibid.*: 262).

7 Although Beethoven was still to write a second finale for Op. 130, Proust is unlikely to have known this very specialised piece of information.

8 Hudimesnil is located on the outskirts of Balbec, an extension of the Guermantes Way.

9 The presence of brass can be inferred from a remark of M. de Charlus (*C*, III: 278). On the basis of Cahier 55, de Souza suggests that the character is actually alluding to the symphony of Vinteuil. It is true that there is no explicit reference to the Septet in the published text at this point and that the context is rather that of the symphony.

10 Even in a later text (1974: 297) he has suggested a link between the number of instruments in the Septet and the existence of seven bedrooms in *A la recherche*. This seems to me to reveal a structuralist bias bordering on the dogmatic.

11 My suggestion has not been taken up in the new Pléiade edition, and it is easy to see why. In the first place Proust took the risk of publishing his novels one by one, so it was impossible for him to make corrections in retrospect. We have to respect the text in the form in which Proust had it printed. Secondly, if such a policy had been adopted, what would the

editors have done with those characters who, towards the end of the novel, die twice? 'It is not possible for us to choose without taking restoration too far' (Tadié 1987: clxxiii).

4   From Vinteuil to Schopenhauer

1 Unless otherwise indicated all emphases within quoted material are mine.
2 I leave aside any systematic study of the hierarchy of the arts in *A la recherche* – architecture, painting, music – which would exceed the limits I have imposed on myself.
3 Henri Bonnet points out that 'épouser' (to espouse) may also be read as 'éprouver' (to experience).
4 Schopenhauer is writing here of Beethoven's symphonies in general.
5 One example among many:

> Only the impression, however trivial its material may seem to be, however faint its traces, is a criterion of truth and deserves for that reason to be apprehended by the mind, for the mind, if it succeeds in extracting this truth, can by the impression and by nothing else be brought to a state of greater perfection and given a pure joy. The impression is for the writer what experiment is for the scientist, with the difference that in the scientist the work of the intellect ['intelligence' in Scott Moncrieff/Kilmartin] precedes the experiment and in the writer it comes after the impression.   (*TR*, III: 914)

I am grateful to David Mendelson for drawing this point to my attention.

5   In Conclusion: Quest for the essence and denial of the origin

1 The reader will have recognised here Molino's semiological theory of tripartition, a theory which I have drawn on in most of my writings.
2 On the complexity of the relationships between these three levels, see Nattiez 1983: 252ff.

References

Abatangel, L. 1937. *Marcel Proust et la musique.* Orphelins apprentis d'Auteuil

Alberti, F.S. 1977. 'La Musique d'Albertine'. *BSAMP (Bulletin de la société des amis de M. Proust et de Combray)*, no. 27, 420–6

Bailey, R. 1968. 'Wagner's musical sketches for *Siegfrieds Tod*' in *Studies in Music History: Essays for Oliver Strunk*, ed. H. Powers. Princeton University Press, pp. 459–94

Bardèche, M. 1971. *Marcel Proust romancier.* Paris: les Sept Couleurs, 2 vols.

Bastide, F.-R. 1965. 'Vinteuil ou Proust et la musique' in *Proust.* Paris: Hachette, pp. 213–25

Beckett, S. 1931. *Proust.* London: Chatto and Windus

Benoist-Méchin, J. 1957. *Retour à Marcel Proust.* Paris: Pierre Amiot, pp. 13–157: 'La Musique du temps retrouvé', reprint of *La Musique et l'immortalité dans l'oeuvre de Marcel Proust.* Paris: Kra, 1926

Bloomfield, L. 1933. *Language.* New York: Holt, Rinehart and Winston

Bonnet, H. 1976. Review of Milly 1975. *BSAMP*, no. 26, 345–7

Boulez, P. 1976. *Conversations with Célestin Deliège.* London: Eulenburg

1986. *Orientations.* London: Faber and Faber

Butor, M. 1971. 'Les Oeuvres d'art imaginaires chez Proust' (1963) in *Essais sur les modernes.* Paris: Gallimard, 'Idées', pp. 129–97

1974. *Répertoire IV.* Paris: Editions de Minuit

Cocking, J.M. 1967. 'Proust and Music'. *Essays in French Literature*, no. 4 (November 1967), 13–29

Coeuroy, A. 1923. 'La Musique dans l'oeuvre de Proust'. *Revue musicale*, vol. 4, no. 3 (January 1923), 193–212

Costil, P. 1958–9. 'La Construction musicale de la Recherche du temps perdu'. *BSAMP*, no. 8 (1958), 469–89; no. 9 (1959), 83–110

Deathridge, J. 1984. 'Life' in J. Deathridge and C. Dahlhaus, *The New Grove Wagner.* New York: Norton, pp. 1–66

Deathridge, J., Geck, M., and Voss, E. 1986. *Wagner Werk-Verzeichnis.* Mainz: Schott

De Lauris, G. 1948. *Souvenirs d'une belle époque*. Paris: Amiot-Dumont

Ferguson, S. 1974. 'Du clair de lune à l'éternel matin: étude du vocabulaire associé à la musique dans l'oeuvre de Marcel Proust'. *Romance Notes* (Autumn 1974), 13–20

Feuillerat, A. 1934. *Comment Marcel Proust a composé son roman*. New Haven: Yale University Press

Guichard, L. 1963. *La Musique et les lettres en France au temps du wagnérisme*. Paris: P.U.F., pp. 230–2

Henry, A. 1981. *Marcel Proust, théories pour une esthétique*. Paris: Klincksieck

1983. *Proust romancier, le tombeau égyptien*. Paris: Flammarion

Laster, D. 1981. Review of Pesson 1980. *BSAMP*, no. 31, 449–51

Lavignac, A. 1905. *Le Voyage artistique à Bayreuth (1897)*. Paris: Delagrave

Lévi-Strauss, C. 1969. *The Raw and the Cooked*, trans. J. and D. Weightman. Harmondsworth: Penguin

Mante-Proust, S. 1946. 'Le Mystère de la petite phrase de Vinteuil'. *Le Figaro littéraire* (13 November)

Matoré, G., and Mecz, I. 1972. *Musique et structure romanesque dans la 'Recherche du temps perdu'*. Paris: Klincksieck

Mayer, D. 1978. 'Marcel Proust et la musique dans sa correspondance'. *La Revue musicale*, no. 318

Mein, M. 1971. 'Proust et Beethoven', *Adam*, nos. 346–8, 18–22

Milly, J. 1975. *La Phrase de Proust – des phrases de Bergotte aux phrases de Vinteuil*. Paris: Larousse

Mounin, G. 1969. *La Communication poétique*. Paris: Gallimard

Nattiez, J.-J. 1983. *Tétralogies: Wagner, Boulez, Chéreau*. Paris: Christian Bourgois

Nectoux, J.-M. 1971. 'Proust et Fauré'. *BSAMP*, no. 21, 1101–20 (includes a letter from Proust to Fauré)

Newman, E. 1933. *The Life of Richard Wagner*. New York: Knopf, vol. 2

1949. *Wagner's Operas*. New York: Knopf

Painter, G.D. 1983. *Marcel Proust: A Biography*. Harmondsworth: Penguin

Persiani, C. 1970. 'Proust, l'opéra et le ballet'. *BSAMP*, no. 20, 994–1008

Pesson, G. 1980. 'Musique et société dans l'oeuvre de Proust'. Diss., University of Paris/Sorbonne

Pierhal, A. 1929. 'Sur la composition wagnérienne de l'oeuvre de Proust'. *Bibliothèque universelle et revue de Genève* (June 1929)

Piette, I. 1985. *Littérature et musique: contribution à une orientation théorique 1970–1985*. University of Namur Press

Piroué, G. 1960. *Proust et la musique du devenir*. Paris: Denoël

Rousset, J. 1962. *Forme et signification*. Paris: José Corti

Schneider, M. 1971. 'Proust et la musique: fervent défenseur de Pelléas'. *Les Nouvelles littéraires* (11 June), 9

Schopenhauer, A. 1909. *Métaphysique et esthétique*, trans. A. Dietrich. Paris: Alcan

1958. *The World as Will and Representation*, trans. E.F.J. Payne. New York: Dover

Société des amis de Proust: réunions sur la musique: 26 August 1956, reviewed in *BSAMP*, nos. 7, 8 (1957–8), 386–93, 538–42; 14 May, 28 August 1960, reviewed in *BSAMP*, no. 11, 424–37

Souza, S. de. 1969. 'L'Importance de la musique pour Proust'. *BSAMP*, no. 19, 879–87

1973. 'Pourquoi le "Septuor" de Vinteuil?'. *BSAMP*, no. 23, 1596–1608

1977. 'Note sur le Pelléas de Debussy et le "Septuor" de Vinteuil'. *BSAMP*, no. 27, 470–3

1980–1. 'Albertine et la musique dans "La Prisonnière" '. *BSAMP*, no. 30, 192–203; no. 31, 367–74

Tadié, J.-Y. 1983. *Proust*. Paris: Belfond

1987. 'Introduction générale' to the new edition of *A la recherche du temps perdu*. Paris: Gallimard, Bibliothèque de la Pléiade, vol. I, pp. i-cvii

Wagner, R. 1981. Libretto for *Tristan und Isolde*, trans. Lionel Salter, Welsh National Opera recording. London: Decca D250D 5

1983. *My Life*, trans. A. Gray, ed. M. Whittall. Cambridge University Press

Wagner, R. and Liszt, F. 1943. *Correspondance de Richard Wagner et de Franz Liszt*. Paris: Gallimard; 2nd edn, 1975

Westernhagen, C. von. 1962. *Vom Holländer zum Parsifal*. Zurich: Atlantis

1963. 'Die Kompositionsskizze zu *Siegfrieds Tod*'. *Neue Zeitschrift für Musik*, vol. 124, no. 5, 178–82

1976. *The Forging of the 'Ring'*, trans. A. and M. Whittall. Cambridge University Press

Yoshikawa, K. 1979. 'Vinteuil ou la genèse du septuor'. *Etudes proustiennes III*, Cahiers Marcel Proust. Paris: Gallimard, pp. 289–347

Index